Let's Talk

Helping Saints Have Better Conversations about Sex

Let's Talk

Helping Saints Have Better Conversations about Sex

Amy C. Jacobs, OTD, OTR/L
Jim R. Jacobs, LCSW, CDWF

CFI
An imprint of Cedar Fort, Inc.
Springville, Utah

© 2024 Amy C. and Jim R. Jacobs
All rights reserved.

No part of this book may be reproduced in any form whatsoever, whether by graphic, visual, electronic, film, microfilm, tape recording, or any other means, without prior written permission of the publisher, except in the case of brief passages embodied in critical reviews and articles.

This is not an official publication of The Church of Jesus Christ of Latter-day Saints. The opinions and views expressed herein belong solely to the author and do not necessarily represent the opinions or views of Cedar Fort, Inc. Permission for the use of sources, graphics, and photos is also solely the responsibility of the author.

Paperback ISBN 13: 978-1-4621-4791-5
eBook ISBN 13: 978-1-4621-4792-2

Published by CFI, an imprint of Cedar Fort, Inc.
2373 W. 700 S., Suite 100, Springville, UT 84663
Distributed by Cedar Fort, Inc., www.cedarfort.com

Library of Congress Cataloging Number: 2024936350

Cover design by Shawnda Craig
Cover design © 2024 Cedar Fort, Inc.
Edited by Julie Irvine

Printed in the United States of America

10 9 8 7 6 5 4 3 2 1

Printed on acid-free paper

Dedication

To all our clients and patients who have allowed us to help and serve them.

CONTENTS

Acknowledgments ix
Introduction xi
What This Book Is and What It Is Not xiii

Chapter 1	Sexual Intimacy versus Sex	1
Chapter 2	Boundaries, Consent, and Agreement	5
Chapter 3	How Often Is Normal?	11
Chapter 4	Initiation	13
Chapter 5	Receiving and Accepting	17
Chapter 6	Connection, Pleasure, Desire, and Arousal	21
Chapter 7	Liking, Wanting, and Expecting	27
Chapter 8	Context Matters	31
Chapter 9	Vulnerability	37
Chapter 10	Resolving Challenges	43
Chapter 11	The Best Sex Ever	55
Chapter 12	Handling Sexual Abuse and Sexual Assault	57
Chapter 13	Pornography, Masturbation, Infidelity, and Betrayal	63
Chapter 14	Conversations about Gender and Sexual Identity	73
Chapter 15	Children and Youth at Church	79
Chapter 16	The Bishop: Leading on Matters of Sex and Chastity	85
Chapter 17	Ongoing Conversations with Children	91

About the Authors 101
Appendix A Speaker-Listener Technique 102
Appendix B Suggested Works of Dr. Brené Brown 104
Appendix C Helpful Resources 105
Appendix D Help for Choosing a Helping Professional 107

Acknowledgments

WE WOULD LIKE TO THANK THE FOLLOWING FOR THEIR CONTRIBUtions to this work and helping support us as we wrote, edited, spell-checked, asked questions, and intruded a bit into your world to see what works: Caralee Frederic, Laura Brotherson, Amy Johnson, Taylor and Sophie Gordon, and Robert McBride.

Introduction

WE HAD ABSOLUTELY NO PLANS EVER IN OUR LIVES TO CREATE A BOOK about sexual intimacy! Even more, we never intended to write a book about sexual intimacy for members of The Church of Jesus Christ of Latter-day Saints! To be honest, as an occupational therapist and counselor who work with many members of the restored Church of Jesus Christ, we have strong feelings about this topic. However, we never thought we had anything worth sharing on a larger scale or in a book. We felt like what we were doing in our work was enough. Helping one couple at a time or one sister or brother at a time was enough for us. We felt like we were doing our part. We were content.

That changed after Jim was invited to speak at a symposium hosted by a local stake in our area. Jim was specifically asked to address the topic of sexual intimacy. He was quite nervous to speak on the topic and felt a little awkward talking so frankly about marital intimacy in the church building. Jim went forward with his presentation and was surprised that his room was standing room only for both sessions.

Well, like anyone, we just assumed "sex sells" and that is why his presentation was so popular! Seriously, however, what happened when the presentation was over changed our perspective on this. Jim had a line of individuals and couples waiting to talk to him after the presentation. The line went all the way from the corner classroom, snaked down the hallway, and continued into the cultural hall. He took comments and questions for over an hour after the symposium ended. He was shocked and unsure how to handle the response.

What was the response? Repeatedly, people said things to Jim like "Why is no one talking about this?" Some said things like "Where were you thirty years ago when we got married and needed this?" Others commented on how this helped them know how to approach the topic of sexuality in their marriage or with their kids. Finally, so many talked of challenges and how they wish they, their spouses, their parents, their children, their Sunday School teachers, and their Church leaders knew about this.

Ultimately, they all had the same question. "When are you going to write a book about this?" They were insistent: "You need to write a book about this!"

What This Book Is and What It Is Not

IN ATTEMPTING TO PUT OUR THOUGHTS INTO WORDS FOR MEMBERS of The Church of Jesus Christ of Latter-day Saints, we want to be clear on our perspectives in this writing. The views and opinions expressed in this book are our own, based on over two decades of experience counseling, coaching, and teaching individuals, couples, and groups about sexual intimacy. These opinions and recommendations are not to be construed, seen, or taken as an official statement of The Church of Jesus Christ of Latter-day Saints or The Church of Jesus Christ of Latter-day Saints Family Services, where Jim has worked for over 20 years. These are our own thoughts, considerations, and suggestions based on our lengthy experience and advanced training, not based on any policies, positions, or programs of the Church or Family Services.

This book also is not a doctrinal exposition explaining the Church's position on any of the topics or subjects addressed in this book. You will not find any official quotes on this important topic. Our goal is not to clarify doctrine, explain a Church stance, or defend any position. If you are looking for doctrine, quotes from General Authorities, or other references, you will not find them in this book. That is not our purpose.

This book is a practical guide to help you talk about sexual intimacy and improve communication about sex in the home, in your marriage, and at church. This book is a heartfelt and prayerful response to the many individuals and couples who, over the years, have asked for help on this topic. After that workshop experience, we have had so many ask for simple help—practical help. People all had this in common—they wanted to know how to talk about sexual intimacy and improve their communication and experiences with sex in their marriages and families. In short, they wanted simple help, easy-to-implement ideas, and tools they could easily put into practice.

So what you will find in the coming pages are simple ideas to help you think and speak about sexual intimacy more easily. You will find things that will help take the fear and embarrassment out of conversations with your spouse and children about sex. Also, you will find help to navigate some of the challenges and current obstacles to sexual intimacy and chastity. We'll start in chapters 1–13 by focusing on couples creating healthy conversations. Then, in chapters 14–17, parents, leaders, and teachers will find helpful hints to better address marital intimacy and related topics in the home and at church. Look for the "Let's Talk" section in each chapter for helpful questions to get you started. Please add your own questions to the list to strengthen your communication with each other!

Chapter 1
Sexual Intimacy versus Sex

A COUPLE ONCE ATTENDED A MARRIAGE SEMINAR TO IMPROVE THEIR intimacy and closeness. While the instructor was teaching them how crucial it is to know what is important to your spouse, he turned to the men and said, "For example, men, can you name your wife's favorite flower?" One husband, reaching over and gently touching his wife's arm, said to her, "That is easy, dear! It is Pillsbury All Purpose, right darling?" And guess who slept on the couch that night?

Intimacy and sex are two quite different things. However, today's world has created confusion about these two topics. Then, because of the strong influence of media, we receive powerful messages about these topics, which can be difficult to decipher. Likely, not one of us on the planet today has seen a realistic portrayal of either sex or intimacy in the media. Yet too many of us get our education from and are heavily influenced by the media when it comes to these topics.

Jim first came to realize that he needed help understanding the differences between these two topics when he was taking the required sexual intimacy course for his degree. He can still remember the first day of the class and the exercise assigned. The professor handed out a paper with fifty or so statements about sex and sexual intimacy. He asked the students to mingle among classmates and find as many people as possible to agree with the various statements on the paper. It was kind of a sex Bingo game.

From Jim: "I was having immense success. I quickly found people who agreed with statements on the paper and jotted their names next to the statements. Frankly, I was not surprised in a class of college-aged adults to find a broad acceptance and agreement with the many different statements. As the time ended, there was only one statement I could not find anyone to agree with. I had all but one!

It was this: "Thinks Danny DeVito is sexy."

This one garnered quite a response from the class. There was only one person in the room who had found someone to agree with this statement. The professor stopped and asked who had agreed with the statement. If my memory was correct, she was an attractive, in shape, young female who most might not think Danny DeVito was her type. (If you do not know who Danny DeVito is, please stop and Google him so you can see!)

She answered the professor in a way I had not anticipated but that indicated she knew something I did not know. She said, "He is sexy to someone!" That young woman got the difference between intimacy and sex. She knew that intimacy was knowing your partner's favorite flower or flour!

Because sexual intimacy truly has many dimensions and levels that go far beyond just marital sex, a strong understanding of the differences between the goals of sexual intimacy and the goals of physical sex is foundational to all the conversations you will have. This small chart may be helpful:

Goals of Sexual Intimacy	Goals of Physical Sex
Making love	Intercourse
Affection and admiration	Orgasm focused
Communication and sharing	Silence, moaning, or screaming
Connection	No connection
Vulnerability	Physicality
Three dimensional (spiritual, emotional, physical)	One dimensional (physical)
In marriage (according to God's law)	Regardless of marriage
Mutual, consensual, and reciprocal	Self-serving (pornography, masturbation, infidelity)

As you can clearly see, there are differences between the goals of sexual intimacy and the goals or acts of purely physical sex. Surely, there are more differences than this simple chart illustrates. However, understanding that sexual intimacy and the act of sex are quite different will be helpful in developing better conversations about sexual intimacy with our partners and our children.

In the coming pages, discussions and help will center on improving conversations and interactions around sexual intimacy. The goal of this book is to help you know how to better navigate this important and wonderful part of marriage. You will learn strategies to improve your interactions and experiences around sexual intimacy. Likely, this will also improve the quality of the sex you are having. Additionally, you will learn to better discuss this vulnerable topic with your spouse and your children. Finally, teachers and leaders at church will learn better ways to support parents in their primary role to educate their children about sex.

Let's Talk
- » What, for you, is the difference between making love and having sex?
- » What did you learn in your home about sex? How does that impact how you view sex and intimacy now?
- » How are intimacy and sex different for you?
- » What can we do to make sex a more multidimensional experience for us?
- » What is the role of connection and closeness in sex for you?

Chapter 2
Boundaries, Consent, and Agreement

As members of The Church of Jesus Christ of Latter-day Saints, we often experience teaching and instruction about the law of chastity and sexual intimacy that gets in the way of the best sexual intimacy in our marriages. It is too common for conversations and lessons about sex to be negative and shame or fear based. Typically, we walk away with messages that may be harmful to good sex in marriage. This can make it difficult for us to know how to talk about sex in healthy and productive ways. It can also get in the way of healthy and loving sexual expression.

All too often, the only message we internalize or learn about sex before marriage is "no, no, no." We understand all the things that are off limits, what we should avoid, and even what we should not be thinking. While this approach may help most young people avoid major lapses with the law of chastity, it can be very problematic for those same young people in marriage. Typically, teaching focuses heavily on the law of chastity and what not to do before marriage. Then, after marriage, there is usually complete radio silence—or at least it can feel that way. We receive a whole lot of guidance as youth and single adults and almost nothing as married partners. So how are we supposed to navigate turning all those nos into yeses? How do we make the shift in thinking that what was once forbidden is now something to embrace?

Getting to "yes!" is important in marriage. We need to come together on a crucial part of marriage and closeness. However, when the focus is on "no" before marriage, most couples have no idea how to get to "yes" after marriage. Most couples are so versed in what is not okay before marriage that they may not have given much thought to what is okay after marriage. Two people coming together with different ideas, interests, drives, and experience are sure to struggle if they do not know how to talk about it. While many couples may figure it out with trial and error and a lot of unselfishness, many have difficulty because they are not prepared to talk about sex. All too many have struggles with lackluster sexual intimacy, boredom, resentment, pornography, and more because they need help to navigate to their best sex ever.

One of the best ways to do this is to have a conversation about boundaries, consent, and agreement. For the couples we help, we approach this by having them visualize a traffic light with its red, yellow, and green lights. Red means stop, yellow means slow down or caution, and green means go. Using this as a starting point can help get a productive conversation going.

First, each spouse makes a red-light list. This is a list of the things that you are not okay with in your sexual contact with each other. This list includes activities, positions, language, locations, and touch that are not okay with this recipient. These are the nonnegotiables, and you will need to discuss them openly and respectfully. If there is something you are not comfortable with for any reason, it should be noted on the red-light list. If you are unsure about what should be on this list, jot down whatever comes to mind. You can update this list over the course of your married life. The goal is to only have the sex that you like. It is perfectly okay for newlywed couples to not be completely sure what should be on this list. It is also completely expected and needed to have things on a red-light list. There should be things we are not comfortable having in our sexual relationship. Having a way to talk about it safely makes this list so helpful. When we can get really clear on what is not okay, it becomes so much easier to explore what *is* okay. Start with what you know and feel, and go from there.

Remember, you will have ongoing conversations, and consent is crucial to a good sexual experience.

Next, make your green-light list. This is the list of all the things you are comfortable with. On this list, the person would write down activities, positions, language, locations, and touch that are okay and desired. On this list, we include all the things that we think would be pleasurable, fun, accepted, and enjoyable. If it is something you want to do, are okay with doing, and feel good about, it should be on the green-light list. Again, if you are unsure, jot down anything you think you would desire. You can always change things in the future.

Lastly, you will complete your yellow-light list. This list contains all activities, positions, language, locations, and touch you are unsure about. If there is something you have heard about, seen in a movie, wondered about, or had an idea about but are uncertain if it is acceptable, put it on this list. We cannot possibly know all the things that are okay and not okay at first. Through this process, you will learn and grow. The yellow-light list is a great place to put things that you are not quite sure about because you have never had the experience before. It is also a good place to put things that may be conditional or occasional. There are times in sexual intimacy where you are okay with something and other times you are not. For example, Jim once helped a couple where the wife was okay with wearing lingerie, but only on the condition that she chose to do it. She struggled with her thoughts and feelings if her husband asked her to wear lingerie. But if she chose to put it on and wanted to do so, then it was okay. Lingerie was on her yellow-light list.

You get the idea here. Each person privately makes his or her own red-, yellow-, and green-light lists. Once each has a good list started, the spouses can sit together and discuss their lists. In this process, each should be sensitive to the other. You are working together to create your couple's red-, yellow-, and green-light lists. Neither partner should pressure, belittle, or coerce the other. The goal is to come together in agreement. Each person should respectfully share his or her list, and each should listen without judgment. The speaker-listener technique is often helpful when doing this.[1]

---

1   See appendix A.

Most couples start with their red-light lists. The rule for this list is that if something is red for one of you, it is now red for both of you. If one of you does not wish to do it, then both people respect it. It becomes part of the couple's red-light list. This is a time for agreement and respect. The green-light list will have plenty of options and activities on it! Clarifying what is not okay can help create freedom, trust, and excitement.

The green-light list is the fun list. This is when the spouses take turns sharing their lists of things they want to do, are excited to do, and are willing to do in marital intimacy. This can be a fun and even stimulating conversation to have as each partner shares the things he or she wants to do, likes doing, and is excited to do together. Marital intimacy should be fun and exciting. If you want to do it, put it on the green-light list. Have fun making the list of all the things the two of you want and like to do together.

Finally, move to the yellow-light list. Here you will talk about anything you are unsure about. The goal of this list is to discuss the things you have not tried but might be willing to try and the things you have mixed feelings about. This list is like a parking lot for things that could become red after you try them. Or after trying something together, it might get a spot on the green-light list. Other items may stay on the yellow-light list because they depend on emotional or environmental circumstances.

After these discussions, you should have a fairly good idea of what is okay and what is not okay. This helps make consent tangible and more obvious. Now, preferences and wishes are out in the open, and you have expressed the things that are not okay for you. You also know all the things—hopefully, a lot of them—that you are happy to explore together and the things that you are unsure about or that may be negotiable.

When couples have these conversations *outside* of the bedroom, in a safe and respectful way, this often helps remove tension *in* the bedroom. When the most vulnerable parts of me are exposed to the most vulnerable parts of you, that is not the time to try to talk about what is okay or not okay. It is not the time to explore things we are unsure about. (Of course, if anything previously agreed on is painful or makes us feel uncomfortable in the moment, we need to speak up right then.) When we establish boundaries we both feel good about, we can come together with confidence and trust. This allows us to focus our efforts on things that are pleasurable for both of us. This kind of connection can feel magical and be the beginning of our best sex ever. The world of sex can be scary. These conversations are like putting a fence around our playground to make sure we are safe to have fun, pleasure, and enjoyment together.

You should update your red-, yellow-, and green-light lists throughout your marriage. For newlyweds, this is the starting point for a list that will evolve over time. You need to plan to continually revisit these lists. Keep them in a private place such as encrypted on a computer or, if printed out, stored in a safe. Items on the red-, yellow-, and green-light lists may shift positions. Changes in health, circumstance, or situation may necessitate moving things around a bit (e.g., aging, injury, pregnancy, sickness, moving in with parents). This should be a living document that is modified to reflect changes over a lifetime. Again, there should never be any pressure or coercion in the ongoing discussion of these lists. The goal is to come together in unity and love! We want to be able to have fun and pleasure while adapting to all the seasons of our lives.

Let's Talk
- » What activities, positions, language, locations, and touch are on your red-light list? Your green-light list? Your yellow-light list?
- » Would you like to explain any items on any of your lists? What would you like me to understand about those things?
- » Is there anything on any of your lists that you feel we need to move to a different list? Have you changed your mind on anything?
- » Are there sexual things we have not tried that you would like to try?
- » Do you get nervous about hurting my feelings when we communicate about what you would like (or not like) sexually? What can we do to make that better?

- » How hard is it for you to ask for what you want when it comes to touch? To sex?
- » Do you ever feel like I push you to expand your sexual boundaries in a way that feels negative to you? What can we do to make that better?
- » Do you ever feel like you need to hold back sexually with me? Please explain.

Chapter 3
How Often Is Normal?

ONE OF THE MOST COMMON QUESTIONS WE GET ASKED IS "HOW OFTEN should a couple be having sex?" Wives may ask their girlfriends to try to find out if they are normal. Husbands might ask their male friends to determine if they are normal or even to brag a bit. Counselors and health care professionals get asked this question all the time. Often, this question has the tone of "Hey, are we normal?" Other times, couples ask this question because they have a legitimate concern or problem impacting how often they have sex. We may feel like there is something wrong with us, our spouses, or our relationships when our desires are not aligned. It is not unusual at all for spouses to have different levels of desire and interest in sex.

Interestingly, most couples have never had any discussion before marriage about how often they want to have sex. Most couples take it for granted or assume it will happen the right amount for them. Hollywood and lack of discussion often lead us to believe an orchestra will kick in with the music so we will know the right time. Typically, sexual frequency is determined by the higher-drive spouse, a wish for spontaneity, or a belief that these magical moments will happen on their own. This is problematic and a common source of contention.

Married couples should not leave the frequency of sex to chance, assumptions, unspoken expectations, or internet searches. There truly is no such thing as a right or normal number of times to have sex. Spouses need to have conversations about how often they would like to have sex as they prioritize this and other needs in their marriage. As with boundaries and consent and agreement, this is an ongoing conversation to address the shifting landscapes of our lives and our sexualities. This is such an easy concept, yet these conversations rarely happen in a marriage.

A simple way to start the conversation is to have each individual take out a sticky note and write down the number of times in a week he or she would like to have sex. Jim has done this hundreds of times in counseling sessions with couples. Interestingly, all the couples he has worked with have written down the same number or range. This was a complete surprise to the couples when they turned to each other and shared the result. Often, the higher-drive spouses were shocked that their partners wanted the same frequency as they did.

Whether or not you chose the same number or range, you can get the conversation going. If both of you said two to three times per week, then you have agreement and can go forward. If one of you said four times a week and another said two times a week, you could compromise and try three times a week. It helps to get what you desire out in the open. Then, you can work from there. The goal is to share your numbers and come to an agreement. Listen to each other, share your preferences for frequency, and then compromise to reach something that works for both of you. Finally, this is not a contract; it is your starting place to help you both experience a mutually desirable frequency of lovemaking in your marriage.

Let's Talk
- » How many times in a week would you like to have sex?
- » What compromise (if your answers were different) works for you?
- » Is there a range that feels more comfortable than a number (e.g., two to three times per week)?
- » Has anything changed in your preferences for frequency of sexual contact? Would you like it more or less?
- » What things affect your level of interest in sex throughout the week? What can we improve?

Chapter 4
Initiation

THIS NEXT SECTION IS SO SIMPLE YET SO PROFOUND IN ITS IMPACT on a married couple and their sex life. Once spouses have had a conversation about desires, boundaries, and consent and have come to an agreed-upon frequency, they need to decide how to initiate sex. Many problems can be avoided by discussing initiation.

This concept often sounds so foreign to married couples, but the implications and power it brings are important. Too many conflicts and difficulties with marital intimacy center on the question of who initiates it. If left to chance, usually the partner with the higher sex drive is the one who feels the full burden of responsibility. This can create all kinds of struggles. This person is likely to feel exposed more often. This person is most likely to be afraid of being rejected. (And, to be honest, if he or she is the only one who initiates, this person *will* feel the most rejection.) On the other side, his or her partner may feel pressured or resentful and may struggle with always being the one who has to consent or decline. We must get past the myth that sex is effortless, easy, and spontaneous. Initiation requires conversation and shared responsibility.

Many power struggles come when couples do not openly address initiation. It is not healthy for one person (either the partner always initiating or the partner always accepting or declining) to be put in that position of power. At any point, either partner is likely to feel nervous, rejected, guilty, shamed, or resentful. To be burdened with always initiating or always accepting or declining is not fair to either partner. This important responsibility (like most responsibilities in a marriage) needs to be shared.

You and your spouse need to have a conversation about who is going to initiate. Let's face it—you are both adults here, and hopefully both of you want to have healthy, fun, and pleasurable sexual intimacy. So you both are responsible for making that happen. We repeat: the two adults here are both responsible for making that happen.

Initiation is often best visualized as a process or system. For example, if spouses want to have sex two to three times per week, they need to decide together how they want to make that happen and how they will share the responsibility for making it happen. There are many creative ways to do this. One couple may choose the "tag-you're-it" method of sharing this responsibility. In this scenario, in a typical week, you have two and a half days to initiate. So, if the husband initiates first, then the wife now has two and a half days to take her turn to initiate. Then, tag! He is it again and the clock starts ticking for him. In this way, the couple would have sex two to three times per week.

Another couple desiring the same frequency of two to three times per week may decide to split the week up. The husband may be responsible for initiating from Sunday to Tuesday, and the wife has Thursday to Saturday with Wednesday being a free-for-all (anyone can initiate). In this way, the couple would have sex at least two to three times per week.

Some couples prefer the scheduled sex approach. This is where you sit down with the calendar and plan which two or three nights this week you will be sexually intimate. Before you balk at this, you might want to try it. Some couples say that sex must be spontaneous and that this approach would take all the fun out of their sex lives. However, many couples who have tried scheduling their sexual intimacy have found that it not only makes sure it happens, but they also think about it more, get excited about it, and plan to make it great! You might challenge the part of your brain that thinks sex needs to be spontaneous. Remember how great you felt when you were dating and planned to do something later in the week? You probably thought about it all week and could not wait for the day to come. Couples who like scheduled sex often describe having wonderful encounters and greater pleasure when the time comes because it is planned, prepared, prioritized, and on their minds!

There are likely many other ways to decide together how sexual intimacy will be prioritized and arranged in the marriage. So be creative! The most important thing is for the couple to fully share responsibility for making sure it happens and initiating it. Please don't leave it to spontaneity and chance. Life is busy and hectic, and we need to make sure this important and special part of marriage is high on the priority list. It is crucial to share initiation and prioritizing. It is crucial neither one of you feel the full burden alone of making it happen. Share the initiation and enjoy the fun!

Finally, it can be helpful to discuss various initiation styles or preferences. We all respond to different approaches. In general, there are five initiation styles or approaches, which are briefly described below. Couples may want to study and talk about what their style or initiation "language" is together and often. Following are the five common initiation styles:

- Provocative-Seductive: This individual wants to see your desire for him or her and wants to feel wanted. He or she may like teasing, seduction, and playfulness.
- Sensual Touch: This individual prefers caresses, cuddling, massage, and physical affection of various types.
- Emotional Connection: This individual prefers sweetness, romantic gestures, connecting conversations, being seen and understood, and demonstrations of love and sharing.
- Sex Talk: This individual prefers being told "I want you" and direct sexual expressions and words.
- Power Play: This individual prefers being approached with confidence and urgency.

Let's Talk
- » What seems like the best system or way for us to share initiation of sex?
- » How do you feel about scheduling sex?
- » How comfortable do you feel initiating sex? How can I make that easier for you?

- » Are you ever unsure about how to initiate sexual intimacy with me? What can I do to make this easier for you?
- » When I initiate sex, how do you usually feel?
- » When you initiate sex, how do you usually feel?
- » Are there ways you would like me to initiate sex with you? What are those things? Please tell me why you like it that way.
- » How would you like us to communicate our sexual needs and desires once sex is initiated?
- » Do I ever misread or misinterpret your initiation of sex? Please help me see the ways you like to initiate sex.
- » What do you think your initiation style is? What do you think mine is?
- » How can I better initiate sex to match your preferred style?

Chapter 5
Receiving and Accepting

HOPEFULLY, YOU FEEL LIKE YOU ARE GETTING SOMEWHERE WITH THE previous conversations so you can set up your sex life in a positive way. Likely you have already had some fun conversations and, if you are already married, are having increased joy in the bedroom. That brings us to the next steps.

Once you have boundaries and agreement, desired frequency, and an initiation approach, you will need to address receiving and accepting. This can be essential to making sure all the above works and works well.

First, receiving and accepting is crucial in any marriage relationship. Sexual intimacy is a very vulnerable thing. You are literally trusting your whole self to another who is trusting his or her whole self—nothing held back—to you. It is a complete union of two people, which is beautiful and sometimes scary. We need to be gentle and accepting. If we are going to set boundaries, establish agreement, and try to be as engaged as possible, we need to be generous in receiving each other. We should try to make saying yes a priority. When both are sharing the responsibility for getting the sex they want, it becomes an almost magical part of the marriage.

So try to say yes! When your partner takes the risk to be open and share, be ready and willing. Please be eager! Be excited! There will always be times when you are tired, feeling unattractive, and unsure you want to do it. However, your partner is putting him- or herself out there. You are going to be putting yourself out there too. The shared risk also needs shared acceptance. When we generously accept each other and our bids for sexual contact, it is a fun experience. Make it a priority to say yes and fully receive your beloved partner. It works well when we do!

Second, there will be times when you will need to alter the schedule, adjust, or be flexible. You will need to have these conversations in advance. This will help you prepare for these inevitable disruptions in a respectful way that is sensitive to the tender feelings of both parties. We need to be sensitive when things get in the way of having the sex we want. These obstacles are things like menstruation, sickness, emergencies, aging, and injuries.

Couples need to discuss how they will handle these things. For example, a couple needs to discuss how they feel about having sexual contact while the wife is menstruating. Some couples may be fine with it and not much will change with frequency, schedule, and initiation. Other couples may prefer to abstain during menstruation for various reasons. Discuss these topics and include them in your agreement. The wife should also have a way to communicate to her husband when these situations arise. Sickness, pregnancy, breastfeeding, unexpected emergencies or injuries, and so forth warrant this same kind of sensitive conversation.

One couple discussed the wife's monthly cycle and decided they did not wish to have sexual contact during the days she was menstruating. Because he may not be aware of when her cycle has started, he needs to know as soon as possible when it is happening. It is not fair to him if he is initiating and does not know he will not be accepted because she is menstruating. It is also not fair to the husband if it is her turn to initiate and she does not because she is menstruating. He needs to know. A couple should discuss how they want to communicate it. One wife, as soon as her cycle started, texted her husband, "Shark Week," and they laughed. Now, they both knew they had to adapt for a bit. Once the husband knew his wife's cycle had started, he strived to be more sensitive and gentle during that week. She felt loved and supported. This is intimacy! The dark chocolate and warm bath helped too!

Couples who are experiencing challenges with injuries, health concerns, and other emergencies should also discuss how to communicate these in advance and with respect and appreciation for one another. A bad back may warrant a quick note or text being sent. An urgent situation for her at work may necessitate a quick call and a conversation over a lunch break. Regardless, a couple needs to decide how to communicate these things. Make every effort to discuss the change in advance, with generosity and genuine appreciation for the love of your partner and the shared joy of your intimate lives together.

Couples experience greater joy in their sexual lives when they discuss these things openly and with respect for the feelings, desires, and needs of the other. If they leave those conversations to chance, all too often feelings are hurt and resentments are built. Be open and agree to communicate changes in advance. In this way, you protect each other and make marital intimacy a shared priority that never gets shoved away. Work together in a proactive way to handle obstacles, setbacks, and the inevitable needs for flexibility and adaptation. Agree ahead of time, outside of the bedroom, how these things will be shared and discussed. When we are generous, accepting and receiving each other can and will be wonderful even if there are speed bumps along the way.

> *Let's Talk*
> » How do you feel about having sex during menstruation?
> » How would you like me to communicate to you that we are not able to have sex according to our planned initiation schedule?
> » How do you like to communicate or show that you are in the mood for sex?
> » What are some good ways for me to inquire about your desire for sex?
> » Do you ever feel rejected by me? What can I do to make it easier for you when I am not in the mood or need to say no to sex?
> » Do you ever feel like you are rejecting me? What can I do to receive no from you better?
> » Do I ever treat you differently when we have not had sex? Please tell me about that and what I can do to better respond to you.

» Have there been any changes in your health or our circumstances that we need to adapt to sexually?

Chapter 6
Connection, Pleasure, Desire, and Arousal

THIS CHAPTER IS GOING TO GET INTO ONE OF THE MOST COMMON areas of interest for couples. There is so much to learn about connection, pleasure, desire, and arousal. The most common reasons couples struggle with each other and the quality of the sex they are having are related to connection, pleasure, desire, and arousal. This chapter will hopefully bring clarity and relief.

First, let us be clear that connection, pleasure, desire, and arousal are different things. Hollywood and social media rarely ever present an accurate portrayal of these four dynamics in sexual relationships. A clear understanding of their differences can be essential and helpful. Let's explore them:

Connection: Did we feel close and connected?

Pleasure: Do we like it or not?

Desire: Do we want it or not?

Arousal: Did you have a physiological or genital response to stimulation?

While this may seem simplistic in nature, it is important that we learn how to distinguish these various aspects of sex, sexual intimacy, and enjoyment.

Connection and pleasure should be the goals of our sexual relationships. We need to move from performance expectations to connection and pleasure expectations. Simply put, we should enjoy the sexual experiences and the sex we are having. Think about the last time you had sex. How was it? Measure it by your levels of connection and pleasure. Did it feel good? Did you enjoy it? Did you feel connected? Cultural expectations and pressures that emphasize orgasm and performance get in the way of the real goal. Aim for your sexual relationship to be one where the desired outcomes are connection and pleasure—the more the better! In these conversations, make sure you are focusing on getting the connection and pleasure you want. Do you both like it? Then do more of the things that bring you both connection and pleasure.

Desire is often the most confusing. Desire is typically what most people worry about and struggle with. This is probably first and foremost because many people incorrectly label sex as a drive. Viewing sex as a drive creates all sorts of stereotypes, confusion, and conflict over what sex is supposed to be and how it works. To be clear, there is no such thing as a "sex drive." Drives are connected to biological needs required for survival (e.g., hunger or thirst). Society and so many of us tend to view sex as a spontaneous drive and wonder why we (or our spouses) have too much or too little of it. We also tend to think something is wrong when sexual feelings and motivations change over time.

Truly, desire is related to motivation. When there is incentive, curiosity, and a safe place to explore, desire comes in response. Most interestingly, sexual desire can be either spontaneous or responsive. Spontaneous desire is what we tend to see in movies or media. This type of desire is probably what leads people to think that sex is a physiological need or drive. This is the standard fare we see played out as normal and expected on our screens. It appears seemingly instantaneously, is often powerful, and invokes strong physiological feelings. Cultural scripts and narratives related to spontaneous desire often create great difficulty for couples. We get the message that we are supposed to automatically want it and if we do not, then something is wrong with us. Even more, society sends the message that men always want and are ready for sex. If he does not, then we think something is wrong with him. On the other hand, women who want sex are often viewed culturally as promiscuous. A woman interested in and excited about sex may feel that something is wrong with her. A misunderstanding of spontaneous desire creates many sexual struggles. Frankly speaking, spontaneous desire is only a small part of the desire we feel sexually.

Responsive desire is a powerful part of sexual desire. Responsive desire is the result of taking steps to create closeness without necessarily feeling desire in that moment. You are creating space for desire to build. If you think and act, the desire will come. It is common for most people to experience responsive desire. When curiosity, interest, pleasure, circumstance, and context align, responsive desire is the result. Too many people believe that something is wrong with them (or their partners) because they do not experience spontaneous desire. Much good would come to many marriages if we learned to understand and normalize responsive desire. While spontaneous desire can be exciting and fun, responsive desire is just as enjoyable and makes for great sexual interaction. When we learn the difference between spontaneous and responsive desire, the sexual pleasure we experience together can improve.

Arousal is often mixed into notions of desire and pleasure. Much harm is done when we are not clear that arousal is not the same as wanting or enjoying. Physiological arousal is a natural response to physical and genital stimulation. Regardless of wanting or desire, genital stimulation may result in arousal. Misconceptions and misinformation here are related to perpetrating sexual abuse and violence. Arousal does not mean anything except that the body has been stimulated. Arousal alone should never be the reason anyone is expected to engage in any kind of sexual interaction. Arousal does not equal desire. Arousal does not equal pleasure. Arousal does not equal consent. Just because someone is aroused physiologically does not mean they "want it" or consent to it. It is crucial we are clear that arousal is only the body's response and is not an indicator of thinking, desire, and pleasure. In short, desire says, "I want to." Arousal simply says, "I can if I choose to do so." Also, it is important to note that for some (usually men), desire precedes arousal and for others (usually women) desire may follow arousal.

Generally, it is more common for men to experience spontaneous desire. Men are often compared to microwaves because their desire often feels urgent, powerful, and intense. Physiological arousal typically follows quickly. On the other hand, women are more likely to experience responsive sexual desire. Women are often compared to slow cookers because their desire and interest often warms up after connection. For women, desire often starts in the head, and women choose it by where they let their thoughts go. Women are often relieved to learn that responsive desire is very normal and is just another pathway to sexual enjoyment. Aging and changes to the body often change these common scenarios for couples. Men, as they age, often experience spontaneous desire less frequently and responsive desire more. This should not be seen as something wrong with them. Women who experience greater spontaneous desire should also never be labeled in a negative way. We should be committed to working together to explore our own levels of desire, pleasure, and arousal. We should recognize there will be unique differences for each individual and couple, and we should not label or stereotype. Because we are living and evolving, we should be prepared to navigate changes as they come.

Married couples wanting to grow in this area might continue the conversations above by exploring the answers to the following questions:

Let's Talk
- » Have you ever felt pressured by me to have sex when you did not wish to do so? When was that, and how can I make sure that never happens again?
- » What helps you want to be sexual with me?
- » Do you think you are more spontaneous or more responsive in your desire? What makes you think this is true for you?
- » What can we do to create an environment where sex is more enjoyable for both of us?
- » Do you think we have a difference in desire? How can we handle that?
- » What can I do to help you feel more ready and interested in sex with me?
- » Do you ever feel pressure to perform to satisfy me sexually? What can I do to help release you from that pressure?

» What can I do to help you feel more comfortable saying yes to sex? What can I do to help you feel more comfortable saying no to sex? (This also could be applied to certain activities, preferences, or actions on the green-light list).[2]

---

[2] Many free marriage and marital intimacy apps have helps for these kinds of discussions. Jim is a certified Gottman therapist. He often recommends the Gottman Card Decks, which pose questions to stimulate conversation around many topics, including sex and sexual intimacy.

Chapter 7
Liking, Wanting, and Expecting

FOR HUMANS, PLEASURE IS A MORE COMPLEX PHENOMENON THAN what other creatures experience. Pleasure in our brains is made up of three interacting and overlapping experiences: liking, wanting, and expecting. The interplay of these factors is interesting and varies for each of us based on our life experiences, especially around touch, pleasure, sex, and intimacy.

Liking is about the pleasure or reward a particular experience, sensation, or opportunity gives us. It can be about what is pleasing to any of the five senses or how we think about and experience an event or activity. *Wanting* is about our motivation, interest, and desire. Wanting is connected to the things we spend time on or pursue. *Expecting* is about learning. Based on previous experience, we come to anticipate what will or will not happen. These three things—liking, expecting, and wanting—play together to influence and impact our sexual experience.

To explain how this might work, Jim likes to use a driving analogy.[3] Imagine that your brain is a car with both an accelerator pedal and two different types of brakes. As you know, the accelerator is what you press when you want to go. You use the brakes when you want to stop. One is for immediate stopping and is usually a pedal near the accelerator. The other, a parking brake, is usually in another location and applied when parked (for example, when parking on a hill). To be

---

3   See Jim's books: *Driving Lessons for Life: Thoughts on Navigating Your Road to Personal Growth* and *Driving Lessons for Life 2: On the Road Again to Better Living, Loving, and Leading.*

even more obvious, an accelerator is something that moves things forward. A brake is something that slows or stops things.

To continue the analogy, when the brain is experiencing pleasure, a person may feel like accelerating, braking, or both. Imagine trying to drive a car when both the acceleration and braking are happening simultaneously. In a car, it is impossible to get anywhere. With people sharing sexual intimacy, it can be the same way if we are not aware of the brakes and the accelerators.

In sex, an accelerator is something that creates excitement and arousal. Sexual arousal could be defined as stepping on the accelerator while releasing the brakes. A car works best when the accelerator is pressed while the brakes are fully released. This is true for sexual intimacy as well (though a bit more complicated!). Accelerators can be thoughts, fantasies, actions, events, touches, and more. For something to be an accelerator, it must be something we like or want, and it must be connected to a positive expectation for pleasure and enjoyment.

In sex, a brake is something that slows down or stops excitement, pleasure, or arousal. In a car, a stuck parking brake can keep any movement from happening. This can be true for sexual intimacy as well. Depression, abuse, certain medications, fatigue, stress, physical health concerns, and more can serve as brakes for sexual interest and pleasure. Like in a car, a sudden hit to the brake pedal can stop sexual pleasure quickly too. Interruptions, embarrassing body functions (e.g., passing gas during sex), and context are a few examples of this kind of sexual braking system. Brakes of both types can and do impact what we like, what we want, and certainly what we expect. Interestingly, most of the things that slow down or stop sexual feelings and responses have nothing at all to do with sex. Stress may be the most common and prevalent brake couples experience that slows down or stops sexual progress and pleasure.

Married couples who are experiencing difficulties sexually may want to explore the areas of liking, wanting, and expecting. You have already laid the groundwork by talking about your boundaries. Your red-light list helped you individually and together to identify what you do not like and will not do. Sometimes, this is enough of a discussion to help couples remove a huge number of brakes. A clear discussion of what is okay and what is not okay often removes many brakes for couples. An exciting green-light list opens the road ahead and helps you step on accelerators. When couples work at keeping their lists up to date, they can eliminate many of these brakes and activate accelerators instead.

Even more, a couple who has worked out desired frequency and fully shares responsibility for creating the sexual encounters they want together eliminates many of the usual obstacles and difficulties around brakes and accelerators. If they are patient with temporary obstacles and are generous in accepting and receiving, there will be many open roads ahead.

You can begin by kindly expressing interest in your partner's likes, preferences, and expectations with a wish to understand and help create more safety in the relationship. Gently exploring what turns you on (accelerators) and what turns you off (brakes) can also be very helpful. The more you understand about each other and your personal thoughts, feelings, and experiences, the more you can work together to get on the road to the pleasurable sexual experiences you want to have with each other.

Engaged couples would benefit from having these conversations during their courtship and well before entering marriage. In a tasteful and respectful manner, couples who are considering and approaching marriage can and should have discussions about red, yellow, and green lights. Relevant personal feelings, thoughts, beliefs, and experiences may also be appropriate to share to help understand each other and better prepare for successful sexual intimacy. Shortly before marriage, these conversations can move to discussions about more specifics, frequency, and initiation. Of course, couples will also want to talk about flexibility and handling the expected bumps along the way.

Let's Talk
- » What are some accelerators, or turn-ons, for you? Would you like to tell me more about any of those things?
- » What are some brakes, or turnoffs, for you? Would you like to tell me more about any of those things?
- » What do you like most about your body?

- » Are there things I do to help you feel good about your body? What else can I do?
- » Are there things I do to make you feel bad about your body? What can I do differently?
- » Are there any parts of your body that you would like me to pay more attention to when we have sex?
- » Do you ever feel like there is an expectation that any touch or affection must lead to sex?
- » Please tell me what parts of sex are pleasurable for you? Are there any parts that are not pleasurable?

Chapter 8
Context Matters

Our world has created so much confusion about sex, sexuality, and intimacy. With the advent of social media, there has been an explosion of information and misinformation about sexual intimacy. Since most of us are consumers of social media, we may struggle to decipher what is helpful and what is not. Media, especially social media, strongly influences our views on many topics, whether we see it, admit it, or know it. This is especially true about sexual intimacy.

One of the main ways media distorts sex and sexuality is to diminish it to just a physical act between two people. While some people clearly act as if this is the case, sex is much more complex than just physical bodies together. Sex is a complex connection of many factors. Understanding these many facets of sex and sexuality is important to creating a healthy and fulfilling sex life that can stand the test of time in a relationship we intend to last forever.

Sexual intimacy is a unique combination of spiritual, emotional, psychological, physical, and historical factors. Both people in the marriage bring a special mixture of these things to their relationship. Whether we like it or not, more than just our physical bodies come to the bedroom when we are engaging in sexual relations with our spouses. These factors can be beautiful when understood and terrible when ignored. We are whole people coming together in a union unlike any other. The very act of sex is symbolic of becoming one. When we fail to take the time to get to know all aspects of our sexual feelings, backgrounds, and perspectives, we miss out on the best sexual experiences ever.

Married couples should have conversations about these various aspects of the "sexuality wheel." It can be exciting to explore together our personal history, background, and perspective on sexuality. Following are some questions that may help you explore the various areas of your sexuality:

Let's Talk
Spiritual
- » In what ways is sexual intimacy a spiritual experience for you?
- » What things do we do to help you feel spiritually connected when we are having sex?
- » Please share with me a memory of a sexual experience that felt spiritual to you.
- » How did your spiritual upbringing affect your views and feelings about sex? How did parents, Church leaders, and others affect that view?

Emotional
- » How does our sexual life make you feel emotionally? What can we do to make it better? Safer? Happier? More exciting? More tender?
- » In what ways does sex help you feel closer to me? Are there ways that sex makes you feel farther from me?
- » What can we do to make our sex life better for you emotionally?
- » What can we do to make our sex life more playful and fun for you?
- » Does sex ever stress you out? Can you please tell me about that?
- » Some people like sex to help them feel close. How is that true for you?

Psychological
- » Many people experience better sex when their minds are engaged. Is that true for you? What can we do to better involve your mind in our sex life?
- » Some people have troubling thoughts during sex. Does that ever happen to you? How can I help you in those moments?
- » What turns you on mentally? What turns you off mentally?
- » How can I help you have the kinds of thoughts you want to have during sex?

Physical
- » How do you feel about your body? What do you like about it?
- » What parts of your body do you not like? How can I help support you when you dislike that part of your body?
- » What parts of your body do you like touched, caressed, kissed, etc.? What parts of your body do you not want touched, caressed, kissed, etc.?
- » What things can I do or say (or stop doing or saying) to help you feel better about your body and sharing it with me?

Historical
- » What does sex mean to you?
- » How does sex make up part of who you are?
- » What did your parents teach you about sex growing up? How does that affect you now?
- » What events or circumstances from your past have impacted how you view and experience sex now?
- » Are there any negative events from your past that we need to talk about so we can avoid repeating anything difficult for you? Would you please tell me about them?
- » Have there been events or circumstances in the past that have confused you about sex, what it means, and how you view it? Please tell me.

These are a sampling of possible questions spouses may want to ask each other. Since this is such a vulnerable topic, it is important to be sensitive. Hopefully, you can see in a quick read of these questions that these factors truly matter and need to be understood. A careful and open-minded discussion can be enlightening. Many couples who gently explore these areas together before marriage and throughout their marriages experience a tenderness that is quite rewarding and enjoyable. Even more, their sexual experiences happen in a context of truly knowing each other and sharing each other. It is so much more than physical bodies.

This concept of context also matters in the day-to-day interactions with each other. We are whole people both in and out of the bedroom. Interactions that may be acceptable and invited inside the bedroom may not be desired and may even be rebuffed outside of the bedroom. When it comes to pleasure and enjoyment, context absolutely matters. It is important that we understand this. Many conflicts around touch and intimacy happen because we fail to consider context. Again, we are whole people inside and outside of our sex lives.

Here is a common example that comes up in counseling settings. You are in the kitchen preparing dinner for you and some friends you have invited over. Your spouse comes up behind you, reaches around you, and fondles your body or swats you on the backside. You react with an irritated and frustrated response. You push your spouse away. Your spouse reacts with confusion and irritation. Your spouse does not understand what just happened and why you are rejecting this affectionate gesture. Your spouse may even respond with something like "But you are so sexy, and I want you" and feel offended by your resistance. There may be tension the rest of the evening because of what happened.

This is a common example of a context problem. When behaviors that are okay in the bedroom happen elsewhere, they might not be accepted because of context. This context interpretation is variable and relates to all factors we considered earlier in this chapter. We need to understand these variables when we engage in physical and sexual contact—especially outside of the bedroom. It is even common to have context factors affect sexual intimacy in the bedroom.

Context that can affect sexual intimacy and the desirability of sexual touch and affection can include mental and physical well-being, relationship characteristics, roles, life circumstances, physical location, and how free you are to play and be spontaneous. The emotional and mental state of your partner can impact his or her interpretation of affection and actions. For example, a spouse who just came home after a long, stressful day at work and a horrible commute may not be ready for an amorous assault right when she walks in the door. Or a spouse who has been home all day with the kids and is wrestling with the baby and cooking dinner when the other spouse comes home may not feel particularly sexy in this moment and may reject advances. When a couple has had a significant conflict and needs time to cool off, one might not be interested in make-up sex, yet the other would find such an encounter healing and helpful. The context matters.

Pregnancy, nursing, living with parents, staying at someone else's home, having a baby in the room, an unlocked door, open windows, being outside, worrying about money, being in a public place, an unclean or un-showered body, and so much more can change the context for an individual and make sexual contact and touch undesirable and inappropriate to them. It is never okay to assume because we are married that all touch in any setting is acceptable. We need to explore context together.

Many couples add this discussion to their red-, yellow-, and green-light lists. You could explore together what kinds of circumstances and situations make something that is typically green now red. You might label some actions as yellow when in certain scenarios or situations (e.g., living with your parents temporarily, staying as a whole family in a hotel room, etc.). Getting clear about how context changes some actions, positions, responses, and situations can be helpful.

You may also benefit from having a conversation about various types of affection and how the context affects the previously discussed elements of liking, wanting, and expecting. Hopefully, it makes sense that what we like in one setting may not be what we like in another. What we want in some situations is surely different from what we may want in a different situation. Certainly, our expectations and experiences can affect this as well. Having a conversation about what we like, want, and expect in various situations can allow us to navigate different contexts better.

You can see how understanding sexual intimacy from a whole-person perspective can help. Taking to your spouse and making sure you are context sensitive can make all the difference. Let us resist the pull of the world to make sex purely a physical act, and let us embrace the wholeness and wonder of who we are in all the places where we are. Our spiritual, emotional, psychological, physical, and historical contexts matter. Partners who are sensitive to all these variables experience greater connection and better sex.

Let's Talk

- » What circumstances or situations would make you not interested in sex or affection from me?
- » Are there times or places where I approach you sexually that make you feel uncomfortable? Can you please tell me more about those times and help me know what I can do better?
- » Are there any things we normally do sexually that you would not want to do in another setting?

Chapter 9
Vulnerability

A FUNDAMENTAL TRUTH ABOUT THIS LIFE IS THAT WE ARE HERE TO connect with others. Everything we hold dear about this life involves connection. We need to connect with God. We need to connect with our neighbors. We need to be connected to our spouses and families to reach the highest aspirations we have for this life and eternity. Connection gives meaning, purpose, value, and joy to this life.

Another truth is the fact that connection with others is difficult. We all want connection and closeness with others around us, but it is scary! When we hunger and thirst for connection, we may also find ourselves overcome by memories of fear, hurt, shame, and heartbreak. All of us have had moments of devastation happen in our lives because of other people. Often, we inadvertently created similar moments in the lives of those we love. Some of our earliest memories and experiences may involve the pain that comes from our interactions with the imperfect people in our lives. All too often, it is the people who are supposed to love us the most who cause us the most pain and difficulty.

On the flip side, most of us have powerful and poignant memories of moments of tenderness, closeness, and joyful connection to another person or group of people. Memories of these pivotal moments with another can shape our world and move us to tears. Powerful, personal moments of closeness and connection with others can be the most rewarding and fulfilling parts of this life. In fact, they are crucial to this life. So why are we not opening up?

We are all indebted to the work of Dr. Brené Brown on this subject. In 2018, Jim was privileged to be accepted into her training program to prepare what she called "Daring Way Facilitators." A select few across the country were given an opportunity to certify in her work and facilitate it. Her work has helped us understand what connection is and what creates it! These things are crucial to understand. They are essential to navigating a close and intimate sexual relationship with our spouses and creating safe moments to teach healthy intimacy to our children and others. What follows comes from Jim's certification and training with Dr. Brown.

Connection requires us to overcome our shame and fear and live in a more daring way. This requires us to be vulnerable. Vulnerability is often feared and misunderstood. Most people view vulnerability as a sign of weakness. We admire people who can be vulnerable, yet we fear to show that same kind of openness ourselves. It has been said that your vulnerability looks like strength to me, but when I do it, it feels like weakness to me. When we are vulnerable, we often feel out of control, and many of us do not wish to feel that way. So we numb our feelings and try to avoid vulnerability. This may protect us from some hurt, but it also shuts off love, joy, happiness, and pleasure. We need to be vulnerable. To be alive is to be vulnerable.

Vulnerability is risking ourselves emotionally when the outcome is uncertain. It is exposing ourselves to the possibility of rejection, hurt, failure, disappointment and more. It is being receptive to life because life is worth it. Vulnerability is where creativity, fun, playfulness, love, and belonging all take root. Vulnerability is to be fully alive. Vulnerability is experiencing the uncertainty of life, knowing there is no guarantee it will work out.

For our purposes, one of the most vulnerable things we can do is trust ourselves to another person during sexual intimacy. Surely nothing may be more vulnerable to us than to share the most sensitive and personal parts of our body with another person. True sexual intimacy is intended to be a full commitment where literally no part of us is held back. This can be frightening. Perhaps it should be frightening. Yet it is also what makes sexual intimacy in marriage fulfilling and wonderful. Few things are more beautiful than when a couple holds nothing back, gives freely, and shares with one another in a trusting and covenant relationship.

Individuals who have learned to be vulnerable have some key things in common. These individuals live life with more courage. They are willing to be imperfect and be seen. They demonstrate greater compassion for themselves and others. These people love themselves so they can love others more fully. Finally, individuals who demonstrate more vulnerability seek authentic connections with others. They have learned to drop the idea that they need to be or act a certain way. They have learned to be themselves. These individuals want to and are willing to be seen, really seen. Dr. Brown has called these individuals "wholehearted."[4]

What stands out the most in these wholehearted individuals, who are willing to be vulnerable, is that they possess a strong sense of worthiness. This is not what we might consider worthiness in a church setting (though that is essential) but a belief about themselves that is transformative. Those who are the most wholehearted and feel they possess the strongest sense of belonging and connection believe they are worthy of it. To believe that you are worthy of love and connection creates love and connection.

How do we get to this place of believing we are deserving or worthy of closeness and connection in our marriages? It is scary to initiate sex and face possible rejection. It is hard to be honest about what you like and what you do not like when it might be laughed at, rejected, scorned, or dismissed. It can be difficult to share inner desires, thoughts, feelings, and wishes with someone else, especially when the topic is so personal and revealing. Our goal is to create a safe space where we feel deserving and worthy of the tenderness and closeness of sexual expression.

Hopefully, you have already received some practical help to get the conversation going. The goal of all these previous conversations is to help create a framework for safe and open conversations about our sexual lives. Likely, if you have acted on some of these suggestions together, you have already found greater connection and closeness. You may have been surprised at some of the tender feelings you felt as

---

[4] See appendix B for suggested works of Dr. Brené Brown.

you talked more candidly about things you like, want, and expect. As you have been direct about your feelings, thoughts, experiences, and upbringing, you may have felt more willing to be vulnerable and trusting in intimate things. This can be the most important part of marital intimacy. The vulnerability required, while both scary and risky, also involves some of the greatest feelings of connection and unity possible in this life. It is truly transcendent and beautiful.

So, in addition to the above conversations, you may need to have some conversations about safety, openness, and vulnerability. Since everything about sex involves being vulnerable, and the best sex requires a high degree of vulnerability, you may wish to explore some of the following questions to better create a strong climate of love and belonging. Even more, we want both spouses to feel they are worthy of love and belonging in the tender intimacies of marriage.

Let's Talk
- » What can I (or we) do to make it safer or more comfortable for you to open up to me?
- » What would make sharing sexual intimacy more joyful, playful, tender, or better for you?
- » What can I do or say to create a more welcoming space for you to open up and enjoy our sex life?
- » Is there anything that I do or say that makes it uncomfortable for you to open up to me about our sex life and the pleasure and connection you want?
- » In what ways could I be more open to you and what you desire sexually?
- » What do I do or say that shows you I want you, I enjoy being with you sexually, and you are fully accepted by me?
- » What can I do to help you feel like you deserve to feel pleasure sexually?

These are just a few ideas on how you might explore together more connection, closeness, and sharing. Remember that each of you will be moving into vulnerable territory. This is a time to be sensitive and listen with your whole heart. This is a time to be gentle with each other and apply your best listening and understanding skills. Even more, this is a time to take a bit of a risk. As you become more open and vulnerable, you will elicit more openness and vulnerability from your partner. This back-and-forth exchange of your inner thoughts, wishes, and desires can create a wonderful pattern of growing closeness, connection, and intimacy. Often this same kind of reciprocal openness creates greater physical pleasure in the bedroom. As we learn together to be truly open, vulnerable, and tender and to hold nothing back, some of the greatest experiences soon follow.

Chapter 10
Resolving Challenges

SINCE EVERY MARRIAGE BEGINS WITH TWO IMPERFECT PEOPLE WITH imperfect histories, imperfect ideas, and imperfect bodies, there are sure to be some expected and understandable challenges to creating the fulfilling sexual relationship you desire to have. Additionally, there is no perfect formula for creating healthy sexual intimacy for a lifetime. You will have many opportunities to grow and change as your lives, circumstances, and bodies change.

We have helped you start conversations to build a strong foundation. We have also added scaffolding to help you build on the basics and create stability and understanding. Even more, we have helped you explore some of the more vulnerable and personal details in your lives that may not seem to have anything to do with sex but actually have everything to do with sex. Hopefully, you have already had some great insights, learned a lot about each other and yourself, and (for those who are already married) had some great sexual experiences. We trust it has been a good experience for you to this point.

Together, we go through many seasons in our intimate and sexual lives. Many of the things you have already learned will help you navigate the smaller challenges. While no book can address all the challenges of sexual intimacy, this chapter will attempt to teach some key principles and discuss a few of the most common challenges to marital intimacy: sex education, lubrication, infertility, sexual disorders, body image, aging, and disability. Challenges such as sexual abuse, sexual assault, pornography, masturbation, infidelity, and LGBTQ+ issues will be handled later in this book. Before we get into specifics, let's discuss some key principles: mutual, consensual, and reciprocal.

This overarching set of principles will help you navigate many of the challenges you will face during the years you will to be intimate and have sex together. These interlocking principles often give couples a great framework to discuss any challenges that may come. The goal of our conversations and our interactions around sex is to discover solutions that are mutual, consensual, and reciprocal. Whatever the challenges may be, if a couple is committed to being one in conversation and connection, they will always find solutions that work for them.

Mutual means you are working together and that both are parties in the conversations, decisions, solutions, and actions. You are a team. Your sexual and intimate life together is something you will cocreate to benefit and bless you for all the years you are together. You should cooperate and coordinate, not compete and conflict. *Mutual* means you are on the same side working together to create the best possible solutions and outcomes for the sex you want to have.

Consensual means you are both fully consenting parties to ideas about, conversations on, and solutions created for your sexual life. While it can mean vulnerability (as we have previously discussed), each party needs permission to speak freely about boundaries, consent, activities, context, preferences, desires, and circumstances regarding sexual activities and connection. As you face challenges together, every solution should be one in which you both can give full consent and truly feel good about. When consensus is the goal, no one will feel pressured, manipulated, intimidated, or shamed into participating. Even more, no one should be harmed in any way (physically, emotionally, spiritually, etc.) as we discuss and engage in sexual intimacy. Sex is best when both people are fully willing and feeling good about saying no and yes.

Reciprocal means we are looking to make the experience pleasurable and enjoyable for both of us. This is not simultaneous orgasms or the unrealistic ideals portrayed by Hollywood and pornography. *Reciprocal*, in this context, is working together to find things that bring pleasure to both parties. A sexual experience may only bring orgasm to one party but still be reciprocal and enjoyable for both parties. Depending on the conversations, choices, and preferences of a couple, their goals do not necessarily need to be based on reaching orgasm. In fact, some of the most enjoyable experiences in your physical relationship together may never involve orgasm. If your shared goal is to create pleasure that is meaningful for both of you, you can often drop the pressures to perform, unrealistic goals, and outcome-based sexual encounters. When we work toward both gaining pleasure from the experience, so much can be enjoyable. It also makes adaptation easier. There are many ways to experience pleasure physically and sexually when we are striving to create shared pleasure. The ideal goal for couples is to enjoy the experience even if the pleasure comes to each in different ways. Sometimes the joy comes from being the giver. Other times it may come from being the receiver. Most often, it is the shared joy of closeness and connection. Couples can discover that sex can be quite enjoyable without necessarily having to receive the same in return all the time. When we focus on the principle of reciprocity, we maximize what pleasure looks like for us.

Put together, the principles of mutual, consensual, and reciprocal can help you navigate many of the challenges you will face as you go forward and create healthy and enjoyable sexual lives together. Let's talk now about some of the most common challenges couples may face.

Sex Education

Many challenges around sexual intimacy and connection would simply be resolved by healthy and appropriate sex education. Most of us are educated about sex from four primary sources: family, school, church, and the internet. This should cause us all to feel concerned. Truthfully, most families—despite the best efforts of Church leaders, experts, and educators—have few, if any, helpful conversations about sex and how to create a healthy sex life. If there were any conversations in our homes about sex, most people remember them as one-time, awkward, and unhelpful experiences. Often, these conversations happen too late in the game, and youth report already knowing (and even doing) the things that a parent awkwardly discusses. These awkward conversations about the birds and the bees rarely ever help anyone have any hope of navigating a healthy sexual life.

School systems may focus more on teaching basic biology, popular ideology, and politically correct things to say and think about sexuality and intimacy. These discussions may not include values, ethics, morals, and frameworks for healthy sexual living and functioning. Often, sex education in the school system creates feelings of awkwardness and more questions when it comes to healthy sexual functioning.

You may have been concerned that churches were mentioned in the places we learn about sex. Churches often facilitate conversations about sex and sexual intimacy. However, those conversations almost always emphasize the things that we should not do. Well-meaning bishops, Sunday School teachers, and youth leaders are often more focused on preventing violations of the law of chastity than teaching the positive and beautiful parts of marital intimacy. Often, children and youth only hear about what is forbidden rather than principles, doctrines, and guidelines that emphasize how beautiful and amazing married sex can be.

The internet is fraught with confusing and mixed messages about sex, sexual intimacy, and more. A Google search by a curious person may elicit millions of confusing messages with no basis in values and no principles or guidelines to evaluate the practices advocated. Additionally, in seconds, one will surely be exposed to explicit, addicting, and harmful articles, pictures, videos, and more. Similarly, scrolling through any social media also exposes that person to countless conflicting images and messages about sex, what is normal, and what should be happening. Most youth and young adults report that most of their ideas and thoughts about sex come from what they see on the internet and social media.[5] This is concerning.

We need to do better at being educated in helpful and realistic ways. (Later chapters explore this for parents, teachers, and leaders.)

---

5   Kimberly J. Mitchell, Michele L. Ybarra, Josephine D. Korchmaros, and Joseph G. Kosciw, "Accessing Sexual Health Information Online: Use, Motivations, and Consequences for Youth with Different Sexual Orientations," *Health Education Research* 29, no. 1 (February 2014): 147–157.

Engaged couples should look for classes, apps, articles, and books that teach helpful ways to discuss and create healthy sex in marriage. All couples should be educated on the differences in male and female anatomy and how each experiences pleasure. It is irresponsible and unwise to enter marriage and a sexual relationship without proper and principle-based sex education. Take charge and find wholesome and helpful resources to discover what you need to know and how to implement it in healthy ways. Be discriminating and seek out the best books, classes, and resources for creating healthy sexuality in your marriage.[6]

Lubrication

Married couples may want to become familiar with and use lubricants. Any sexual activity that lasts for more than about four or five minutes (and we hope that is your goal!) would benefit from lubrication. Lubrication, or "lube," becomes more important as we age and our bodies change. In short, become familiar and comfortable with lube. Experiment with different products and find those you like. Here is a quick review of the three most common types of lubrication:

- Water-based: These are less irritating to the skin but can dry quickly and get very sticky.
- Oil-based: Often made of things like coconut oil, oil-based lubricant can be very effective. However, most oil-based lubes are not compatible with latex contraception and may be harmful to sheets, clothing, and other materials.
- Silicone-based: These are waterproof and long-lasting, and they dry without stickiness. They can be used with latex contraceptives.

Infertility

Infertility may be one of the most difficult challenges for married couples. For members of The Church of Jesus Christ of Latter-day Saints, it can be especially difficult due to our emphasis on families, large families, and eternal families. Couples who are experiencing

---

6   See appendix C for some suggestions and resources that may be helpful.

the challenge of infertility should seek professional help from doctors, counselors, and other experts on this issue. Individuals who know they may be unable to have children should discuss this openly and sensitively with potential marriage partners. Couples should handle these issues with respect and dignity when discussing them.

When it comes to sexual intimacy in marriages where infertility is an issue, some common challenges arise for couples. First, sex can become outcome based. Many couples struggling with becoming pregnant find their sexual lives turning into a science experiment. Temperatures, calendars, and ovulation tracking apps can quickly make sex unfulfilling and more of a burden or chore. Couples who are facing this challenge should have open conversations about how to ensure their sex lives do not become mechanical, routine, or like a laboratory. Be honest and discuss the challenge. There are many ways to keep sex fun, even when it might seem somewhat like a science experiment.

Second, when the struggle with infertility arises, some couples find that sex becomes only about having children. While this can happen for any young couple, it can be especially common in couples with challenges in conceiving a child. It is important to have the conversations previously mentioned and discuss both aspects of your divine sexual powers. Sex is for procreation, but it need not be only for this purpose. Couples need to discuss how they can protect their sex lives from becoming just about having a child.

Third, couples who are experiencing infertility, and are unable to have the children they want, may begin to feel resentment. They may feel like their bodies are broken or defective. They will surely experience a mix of hard-to-manage feelings including anger, resentment, grief, loss, frustration, and depression. Individuals and couples should be willing to discuss these things with each other and seek professional help. Separating our sex lives from the challenge of infertility can be difficult, but it is not impossible.

Sexual Disorders

Sexual disorders tend to fall into two categories: desire and dysfunction. Simply put, if you do not have the desire but have the function or the ability, then you have a desire problem. If you have the desire but not the function, then you have a physical dysfunction. *Desire* means "I want to," and *physiological function* means "I can." Understanding whether the problem is one of desire or dysfunction is crucial to resolving the challenge. In these discussions, it is important to remember earlier discussions on spontaneous versus responsive desire when considering if there is a problem. Again, responsive desire is a significant part of the sexual experience for most women and many men.

First, some basic education—it is normal for men to experience varying levels of ability to have an erection over their lifetimes. Stress, aging, health problems, and medication often affect this ability. Because of societal pressures and messages about manhood, men often become depressed and discouraged when they are not able to have or maintain an erection. Men should seek medical help first and do all they can to address any physical health concerns that may be affecting sexual ability. Men should not be embarrassed or ashamed about changes in this area of life. Most problems, if addressed early on, can be solved. Schedule an appointment with a doctor sooner rather than later. You will be glad you did. Please be willing to seek help for your and your partner's sake.

Second, since we're talking about men here, it is crucial to know that most experts say men, on average, can only engage in sexual intercourse for about four minutes before orgasm. Contrary to portrayals in movies and pornography, four minutes is normal. Too many men and women think a man has problems with premature ejaculation if he cannot go for longer periods of time. If you are ejaculating after two to eight minutes, you are probably normal. If this concerns you, talk to your spouse, see a counselor, and learn together about techniques and strategies that can help you last longer during sexual intercourse. Some of these strategies are fun and can be quite enjoyable as a couple works together to delay climax.

Third, moving to women, it is now known that women require clitoral stimulation in order to have an orgasm. As scientists and others learn more about women's bodies, it is evident that all orgasms for women come from clitoral stimulation. Women need eight to twenty minutes of direct stimulation to the clitoris to reach orgasm. Most women cannot have an orgasm during or from sexual intercourse. The clitoris must be stimulated in some other way. Couples need to be educated and include this in their conversations about their sexual activities. Women should never pretend to have an orgasm to solve challenges. This is dishonest and perpetuates problems. Usually, openness and education are all that couples need in this area. Because a woman needs more time to reach orgasm than a man, couples should discuss how they will address this. Also, please do not forget earlier discussions on responsive desire that so often apply to women and their sexual response. Connection and responsive desire often impact her sexual response and pleasure.

Finally, couples should discuss any difficulties around sexual intimacy. If the problem is desire, couples should set aside time to talk about what is going on in the relationship and in life. They should explore the reasons why either one or both are not interested in sex. While a decreasing desire is normal over a lifetime, a complete lack of desire often indicates other challenges like stress, depression, relationship conflict, or other overwhelming issues. Often couples can talk these things out. Any experiences of pain or discomfort are important to discuss. Individuals and couples should be willing to seek professional help for these issues. Resolving issues that impact desire and pleasure is important for your relationship and your health.

If the issue is one of function—meaning the body is not responding—individuals and couples should be respectful to each other in their conversations and interactions. It is interesting that many women blame themselves if their husbands cannot get or maintain an erection.[7] She assumes it is because something is wrong with her. At

---

7   Kate Pickles, "What Women Think about Erectile Dysfunction: Nearly Half Blame Themselves When Their Partner Can't Perform between the Sheets," *Daily Mail*, February 12, 2016, https://www.dailymail.co.uk/health/article-3444460/What-WOMEN-think-erectile-dysfunction-Nearly-half-blame-partner-t-perform-sheets.html.

the same time, men feel broken or defective and blame themselves. Likewise, men's greatest desire is to please their wives sexually.[8] When they fail at this, they feel even more discouraged and broken. To help resolve these challenges, set aside time to discuss what is going on and share your thoughts and feelings about the challenge. The topics previously discussed in this book can help make this safe. If the problem is clearly not one of desire, seek professional help for issues of function. There are almost always medical or other concerns that warrant intervention. Please seek out a good medical provider, counselor, or sex therapist as soon as possible. Be willing to ask for help. Almost all problems of function can be resolved.[9]

Body Image

Developing and maintaining a healthy body image is crucial for healthy sexual enjoyment and functioning. Criticizing our bodies and focusing on what we do not like about them is associated with difficulties in all areas of our sex lives (e.g., desire, fun, safety, pleasure, orgasm, etc.). While this challenge is more common in women, men are also susceptible to poor body image. We can overcome this challenge by accepting that the Lord has created a variety of beautiful bodies in all shapes and sizes. We need to do all we can to challenge societal pressures and messages about body shape and size and embrace the skin we are in. We need to learn to celebrate more of what our body already is rather than what society or others say it should be. Although what society says about our body shape and size may never change, we can create our own healthy narrative. We should do all we can to embrace our bodies and keep them in optimal health with regular exercise, healthy diet, adequate sleep, and so forth. Then, we should learn to embrace each other's beautiful bodies and enjoy that awesome privilege and experience. If you are struggling with poor

---

[8] Marc DiJulio, "Male Sexuality and Emotional Needs," *Innovative Men's Health*, https://innovativemen.com/blog/male-sexuality-and-emotional-needs.

[9] Please see appendix D for suggestions on choosing a provider, counselor, or sex therapist.

body image or negative self-talk about any part of your body, please seek professional help as needed.

Aging and Disability

Many of the former chapters have provided help to address the challenges inherent in aging and disability. A couple generally experiences enjoyable sex throughout their lives together when they (1) have ongoing conversations about red, yellow, and green lights; (2) are talking about likes, wants, and expectations; and (3) are open about what has changed and how they want to address it. A married couple should never give up on creating a healthy intimate life together because of aging or disability.

Aging can create many opportunities for creativity and adaptation. If a couple has been having ongoing conversations about their sex life, often they are already versed in making small changes to make things better. Be willing to adapt and adjust as your bodies change. Rediscover the concept of responsive desire. This becomes even more important as our bodies age. Most couples continue to have satisfying sex lives well into their advancing years. Keep talking and never give up.

Disability can affect sexual function and sexual desire. Work with medical providers to understand all challenges regarding function, and work together to resolve any that you can. The stress and challenge of disability can often affect desire. Counsel with each other and professionals to resolve any stressors, pressures, or difficulties around desire. Many individuals with physical disabilities continue to have strong desire and satisfying sex lives. Never assume that a disability has taken away desire and interest. Be open and discuss it. When it comes to performance and positions, consider working with an occupational therapist to help learn how to make adjustments and adaptations. A good occupational therapist can help you consider positioning, pillows, and adaptive equipment for enjoyable sex.

Please know that it is normal over the course of life and sometimes with disabilities to have decreased sexual intercourse. There are many other aspects of physical touch, closeness, and connection that are satisfying to married couples. Many couples find exploring touch and stimulation to be very helpful when aging and disability have affected the ability to have sexual intercourse.

Finally, mental and emotional struggles can be disabling and often have an impact on sexual health and functioning. Many medications used to treat mental health conditions have the common side effect of creating problems with sexual desire or function. Talk to your doctor about any changes in desire or function because of medication. Many options are available to treat mental health conditions while not impacting sexual ability and desire. Be willing to speak to a counselor if your mood, medications, or mental health challenges are affecting your sex life. You owe it to yourself and your spouse to do all you can to address those challenges together.

As you can see, there are many challenges and common obstacles to a fulfilling sex life. You and your spouse can navigate most of these by seeking education, having open and loving conversation, and working together. You can also see that seeking professional help is important. Be willing to turn to each other and qualified and sensitive professionals to resolve these and other challenges as they come. There is much that can be done to have a sexually fulfilling relationship throughout our whole lives.

Let's Talk
- » Do you think it would be helpful to take a sex education class together or read a book together about sexual intimacy? Please tell me about that.
- » What do you wish I knew more of in terms of your body and what helps you feel pleasure? Will you teach me more about how your body works?
- » What does an orgasm feel like for you?
- » Would it help you more if I asked you what you want and need?
- » What impact do you feel like Church teachings had on your views of and experiences with sex?
- » Do you ever feel like something is wrong or not working with your body? Please tell me more about that.

- » Some people feel ashamed or guilty when they cannot perform sexually or have an orgasm. Do you ever feel that way? How can we handle that together?
- » Have there been any changes in your health that you feel are impacting us sexually? How can we handle those better?

Chapter 11
The Best Sex Ever

WE HAVE TAUGHT YOU MUCH ABOUT HOW TO CREATE A HEALTHY sexual life together. Our discussions have put the foundation and scaffolding in place for you to have healthy conversations about your sex life. You have learned to better understand each other's thoughts, feelings, desires, and backgrounds. You have learned to identify and face challenges that may come. The goal of the previous chapters was to get to this point. However, what is it that creates the optimal sexual experience for couples? What attributes do sexually successful couples have that make for great sex? Here are some key points you may have already realized from previous chapters. We are including them here to help you create and maintain those things that make for the best sex ever!

The best sex ever is created by couples who do the following:
- Have ongoing conversations over their lifetimes.
- Focus the conversation more on connection and pleasure.
- Challenge any ideas, thoughts, or beliefs that sexual pleasure in marriage is a sin.
- Become close friends who enjoy each other.
- Spend time together and give each other attention, lots of affection, and plenty of sex.
- Stay present, focused on, and fully engaged in what is pleasurable for each other.
- Be authentic, curious, willing to explore together, and willing to take some risks to find what works to create sexual pleasure.

- Have no expectations for certain sexual outcomes (e.g., orgasm), but stay playful, fun, spontaneous, creative, and focused primarily on pleasure.
- Strive to be responsive, committed, and accessible to each other.
- Prioritize sex and create sex worth having.
- Be vulnerable, empathetic, and willing to give and receive.
- Turn toward each other, have fun together, play together, and engage in ongoing bids for connection.
- Want it, believe they are worthy and deserving of it, and regularly and consistently work at it and communicate about it throughout their lives.

Let's Talk

» How do you feel we are doing in this area?
» How do you feel about the level of connection we have during sex?
» In what ways can we increase connection and pleasure for you?
» What can we do to make our connection more intimate for you?
» In what ways do you think we might be focused more on physical sex rather than connection and intimacy? What can we change or improve?
» Is our sex life enjoyable and fun for you? What can we do to make it better?

Chapter 12
Handling Sexual Abuse and Sexual Assault

Sexual abuse and sexual assault are two of the most destructive and devastating things that can happen to anyone. Sexual abuse of any kind can create many challenges for individuals, marriages, and families. Sexual abuse of any kind should not be tolerated. We should make every effort to prevent, stop, and report any sexual abuse happening in our homes, our families, and in our communities. It is a terrible evil, and we need to all do more to protect children, women, and men from it.

Since this book is more about how to have conversations about topics that impact our sexual lives, we will not delve into all the possible consequences and challenges associated with sexual abuse. The goal here is to help couples be open about any sexual abuse that has happened and learn how to navigate around and through it to create a healthy sexual relationship. We want couples to be able to talk about it, create solutions, and develop a relationship where sex can be enjoyable and positive. Often, a sensitive spouse, safe and healthy ongoing conversations, and tender exploration can facilitate healing for a victim of sexual abuse.

First, and perhaps most important, sexual abuse victims are *never* responsible for the abuse. They did not want to be abused, ask for abuse, or put themselves in situations where they chose abuse. It is a terrible wrong to blame victims for any type of sexual abuse perpetrated on them. We all should be careful to never blame, suggest accountability, or shame people by making them believe it was their fault they were abused. Partners should be very tender, sensitive, and empathetic when learning about any sexual abuse that may have happened to a loved one. Loved ones need to be fully heard, accepted, and embraced for having endured something so terrible. Be sensitive, listen with love, and offer compassion and empathy.

Second, sexual abuse in all its forms may create difficulty with trust, especially concerning sex. Seriously dating couples should discuss any abuse history and how it has affected them. They should have an honest discussion without details so each person can be aware of the past and how it might affect a future sexual relationship. While it is not possible to anticipate all the ways sexual abuse may affect future relationships, creating openness and safety to talk about it is the first step. Have this conversation while dating, and be determined to continue it as soon as you are married and throughout your lives.

Third, people who have been abused sexually may have, understandably, expected and unexpected struggles with physical affection and sexual intimacy. The earlier conversations about boundaries and consent are even more important in situations where abuse has happened. Partners need to be extra attentive and sensitive to the red- and yellow-light lists and watch for signs of discomfort or struggle. Since we cannot anticipate all the things that might be difficult, couples often find it helpful to have an additional way to communicate in the moment when something triggers or creates difficulty for the person who was abused. Many couples create a safe word or code word that indicates thoughts, feelings, or memories from the sexual abuse have been triggered. Other couples have an agreed-upon safe touch that indicates the same. For example, Jim worked with a couple where a touch on the upper arm communicated they needed to stop whatever they were doing because memories from the abuse had been triggered. Some abuse victims may not be able to speak in triggering moments. A safe touch can often communicate the struggle. Some couples use both a safe word and a safe touch.

Partners need to learn about body language cues and signals that may indicate their loved ones have been triggered. Examples of possible indicators that experiences from the abuse have been triggered may include (but are not limited to) crying, spacing out, pushing away, becoming angry or irritable, avoiding eye contact, and more. Sensitivity in the moment can help the partner stop or slow the action to create an environment of safety, concern, and empathy. Conversations outside of the bedroom about these moments can help couples explore ways to manage them should they arise again. Identify any words, actions, positions, or events that might be triggers, and learn to work around them. Partners need to exercise extra care never to shame their spouses for these reactions. They are involuntary and caused by the trauma of abuse. The partner does not choose these reactions and responses.

Sexual abuse is often developmental in its effects. What this means is that the consequences of sexual abuse often show up during the normal development of a person. It is not unusual for a sexual abuse victim to feel healed and be certain the abuse is in the past and then have it show up with different or similar effects in key moments later in life. It is also not unusual for an abuse victim to have struggles at the time of marriage, at the birth of a child, when a child reaches the same age as they were when they were abused, and so forth. Couples should anticipate that the abuse from the past may show up in different ways throughout the course of their lives together. This is normal. Ongoing conversations become even more critical. Couples where one or both have an abuse history should prioritize regular conversations about their sexual lives that include conversations about abuse. They may choose to add questions like the following:

Let's Talk
- » Has anything recently triggered feelings of powerlessness, helplessness, or abuse?
- » Is there anything that I am doing, or we are doing, that is triggering any thoughts, feelings, or memories of your abuse?
- » What can we change or improve to make touch, affection, and sexual intimacy safer for you?
- » Do you ever feel pressured by me sexually? When are those times, and how can we create safety for you? How would you like to tell me that you feel unsafe or that feelings, thoughts, or memories of sexual abuse have been triggered?

» When your thoughts or feelings from the abuse are triggered, how would you like me to respond? Would it help if I held you?
» What do I need to know about your sexual abuse experience that would help me be more sensitive and supportive of you?

These questions (and others) can facilitate ongoing conversations where we build trust and safety over time. A responsive partner who really listens and responds creates safety. Over time, the abused spouse can learn that this relationship is safe, tender, and healing. What was once difficult can be safely healed through tender conversations and expressions of physical safety and intimacy.

Individuals who have been sexually abused should seriously consider counseling. Even if you had counseling in the past, returning to counseling can be helpful as you experience the new vulnerability of an active sexual life. Often, the expected vulnerability and openness natural in married sexual life creates new experiences that may trigger memories of the abuse. This does not mean you did not heal or that previous counseling was unsuccessful. This just means there are new challenges that you could not have possibly addressed in the past. A counselor experienced with treating sexual abuse and trauma can be very helpful in navigating the new experiences and additional triggers or challenges. Spouses should be willing to participate in counseling to learn how to be more sensitive and better navigate any issues that arise. Again, open dialogue with each other is crucial.

Some abuse victims have difficulties with sexual desire, arousal, and functioning. As stated in the chapter on resolving challenges, these should be addressed. Desire problems may be connected to the trauma and residual feelings from the abuse. Couples should discuss these problems with each other and seek help from a qualified counselor. Discuss problems with arousal and function with a medical provider or counselor.

Finally, supportive loved ones should be careful to never make assumptions about abuse and its effects on their partners. We should be cautious to never rank abuses on some arbitrary scale of severity or compare it to other types of abuse. All abuse is destructive. We need never conclude how someone should have reacted because of the abuse he or she endured. The practice of comparative suffering is never helpful to victims of abuse. We should strive to be warm and empathetic and listen more than we talk. Then we can be gentle and curious about how the abuse affected them. It does not matter how other people experienced abuse. All that matters is what your partner experienced and helping them through it.

Chapter 13
Pornography, Masturbation, Infidelity, and Betrayal

AS HAS BEEN MENTIONED PREVIOUSLY, THE PURPOSE OF THIS BOOK is to offer practical suggestions to have better conversations about sex. No book with this stated purpose would be complete if there was not a chapter on pornography, masturbation, infidelity, and betrayal. Also, like in previous chapters, the discussion will center on having conversations about the above. There will not be much content about the evils or perils of these practices. We are going to assume that members of The Church of Jesus Christ of Latter-day Saints are already clear that these practices are considered sins and are not ones we should accept or participate in. Members of the restored Church of Jesus Christ have many sources to which they can turn for help to understand the evil nature of these practices.

Conversations about pornography should begin from the birth of a child. Because we live in such a sexualized world, children and families should be openly discussing media, its content, and its intent all throughout children's lives. This should include conversations about music, pictures, videos, GIFs, literature, audiobooks, websites, apps, manga, comics, conversations, chat rooms, television shows, movies, video games, and more. There is seemingly no end to the ways the adversary can distribute false, degrading, explicit, tantalizing, and destructive messages about and depictions of sex and sexual expression.

Conversations should also cover devices, including phones, computers, laptops, tablets, listening devices (e.g., smart speakers), personal digital assistant devices, gaming consoles, and more. In some cases, discussing things like adult bookstores and websites, strip clubs, massage parlors, escorts, call girls, dating and hookup apps and websites, prostitution, and sex trafficking may also be necessary. All these sources and devices (and surely more) can be used to access inappropriate content and engage in inappropriate behavior. We no longer live in a world where one must seek sexually explicit content and activities. We live in a world where it seeks us. So we need to be talking about it as much as, if not more than, we are digesting it from the myriad of sources around us.

We should make every effort to keep these conversations positive and centered on correct teaching, loving discipline, and full support. Conversations that are punitive, shaming, degrading, or full of hostility, disgust, or animosity are never helpful. The best way to respond to any of these inappropriate actions is with loving connection. Strong and loving connection with ongoing conversations and appropriate affection are the best protectors against struggles with pornography and other actions. As with almost anything, the answer starts with loving kindness and charity. Unfeigned love is crucial to overcoming any exposure or struggle with these behaviors.

It would be wise to remember there are various levels of exposure and contact with explicit materials and behaviors. We should be careful not to label accidental exposure or curiosity as sinful. We should also not be too quick to label intermittent use or a wrestle to stop viewing or accessing materials or engaging in behaviors as addiction. Generous and loving guidance, open communication, and proper teaching are the best and first ways to help. If needed, meeting with the bishop, participating in addiction recovery, and seeing a counselor may also be appropriate.

When someone you love has disclosed or been found to have a struggle with inappropriate materials or behaviors; it is best to respond with loving-kindness. This may feel impossible, especially when you and this individual have not had ongoing conversations or if he or she has been dishonest and deceptive. Your initial reaction may include shock, anger, disgust, pain, disappointment, and fear. Therefore, your conversations on these topics should often be held at a time different from the discovery or confession. This may make it easier to respond with compassion and gratitude that the behavior is no longer hidden. Parents and partners should arrange a time to discuss when minds are fresh and hearts are more receptive. Keep these conversations positive. The goal is to express love, understand the challenge, and work together for loving solutions. Individuals who are struggling should be prepared (and in the case of children, encouraged) to be candid and willing to disclose the full nature of their challenges. Partners and parents should be ready to discuss any feelings of shock, hurt, betrayal, disappointment, and so on.

Parents, spouses, and family members should never feel like they are responsible for their child or loved one's behavior. Even more, supportive loved ones should not view themselves as the ones to cure or stop the problem. It is not your fault. You did not cause it, and you cannot cure it. However, you can help by surrounding this loved one with generous support, encouragement, proper teaching, and unfeigned love. Those who are struggling need to assume full responsibility for making the changes they need to make to stop this behavior and address all its consequences. Ongoing conversations that are loving and focused on solutions are the best way to facilitate healing for both parties. Parents and couples should be willing to seek help from leaders and professionals to help these conversations be productive and healing.

Couples who are seriously dating should include conversations about pornography, masturbation, and any other related challenges. There should be no assumption that only men engage in these behaviors. Both should be prepared to inquire about and share their experiences and contacts with sexually explicit materials and behaviors. The goal is to understand and support each other. Do not share explicit details about the materials or actions, but gain an understanding of when and where there has been exposure, how much it has happened, and what is currently happening. Partners who are having doubts about marriage because of these conversations should be prayerful and honest about these doubts. It can be helpful to talk to parents, family members, Church leaders, and professional counselors about these feelings before making decisions.

In parent-child relationships, in dating that is moving toward marriage, and in marriage, establish a regular schedule of conversations about this topic and the challenge to overcome it. An individual who has been forthcoming and is talking about it wants help; he or she needs loving support and assistance. Scheduling regular, ongoing check-ins (e.g., a family council) can be helpful. Having regular conversations can eliminate a lot of challenges that are typical in the struggle with explicit media or inappropriate sexual behaviors. A regular meeting benefits both parties. The struggler knows there is support and loving conversation. He or she never has to struggle with rationalizations, fear of being shamed or rejected, or trying to come up with the "best" time to talk about it. The supporter feels less betrayal and has less anxiety because there is a set time to address the challenge, and he or she does not have to wonder whether it will be discussed. The struggler should be honest and avoid sharing details. The supporter should be open, attentive, and gracious. As each party seeks to understand the problem, they can work together toward solutions. The supporter should help the struggler discuss the frustration, shame, and difficulty he or she experienced. Likewise, the struggler should give the supporter time to discuss any feelings of betrayal, anger, frustration, stress, and disappointment. Here, the struggler must listen without defensiveness, rationalizations, or blame and seek to truly understand the supporter's feelings. Honesty on both sides is important.

Once both parties feel heard, the discussion should move to learning from past mistakes and seeking to understand thoughts, feelings, and experiences associated with the last use or behavior. Then, the parties involved should move quickly to create a plan for the next time. The individual who is struggling should create a plan to implement the next time he or she is tempted. When we shift our focus to learning and creating a plan, we also shift our focus to solutions. We can remove the shame and hurt as we focus on a plan that can be modified to prevent future use. Parents and partners should never create or impose plans upon their loved ones. They can help brainstorm ideas, always encouraging the struggler to take ownership and put the plan to work. When we focus together on creating plans to be free, we make progress. It also helps because we live in a world where technology is changing so rapidly. We need living plans, discussed kindly and frequently to better address the rapidly shifting landscapes of available explicit content. Realistically, every one of us should be having open conversations in our homes, our dating, and our marriages about things we can and are doing to manage exposure to explicit content. The more open, engaging, loving, supportive, and proactive these conversations are, the better. Frequency should be determined by each unit, but these discussions must be consistent and always loving. The goal is to get to "Us against the Problem." A team approach works best!

Individuals who continue to struggle while having loving and supportive conversations with parents, partners, spouses, and Church leaders should be encouraged to participate in addiction recovery programs and groups. Addiction recovery groups are an effective part of a plan to overcome these types of struggles. Support groups for parents and spouses are also available. Be willing to participate fully and regularly. Many have found hope and healing in 12-step groups and programs. You can also enlist the help of professional counselors to address all aspects of compulsive and addictive cycles. Be careful and discriminating as you choose a counselor who has similar values or demonstrates support and help for you within your values.

For married couples, when exposure to sexually explicit material has moved to live interactions (of all the various types), conversations should continue to be loving and supportive. In these cases, both parties should be meeting with ecclesiastical leaders, engaged in addiction recovery programs and groups, and participating in counseling. Counseling should include both individual and marital counseling. Connect with counselors who have experience with infidelity and betrayal trauma. These counselors have unique training to address the many complex factors that accompany these kinds of struggles. They are prepared to navigate you both through the path to recovery and healing. Partners should be careful to continue to engage in good health practices spiritually, mentally, physically, socially, and emotionally. This is a time where more support and healthy practices are needed the most. Do not neglect yourself as you face these challenges together.

Let's Talk (for couples)
- » Please tell me about your past experiences with pornography.
- » How was pornography addressed in your family growing up?
- » What actions have you taken to stop or prevent viewing pornography?
- » Have you ever wondered if you were addicted to pornography? What makes you think that?
- » What is your personal plan for maintaining virtue and staying away from explicit content?
- » What steps are you willing to take to keep pornography out of your life?
- » Have you ever been involved in online relationships (including anonymous web chats), exchanged explicit videos or pictures, or visited places like strip clubs? Please tell me about those experiences and how they impacted you.
- » What are your thoughts about romance novels or erotica? Please tell me about your experiences with reading sexually explicit material.
- » When you find yourself struggling with pornography and explicit material, what is your plan for telling me about those struggles?
- » What can I best do to support you when you are struggling?
- » How do you want me to tell you about my struggles with pornography?
- » What can I best do to support you when you learn I have been struggling?
- » How do you feel about my relapses with pornography? What can I do to help you with those feelings?
- » Some spouses feel betrayed when they learn that their partners have relapsed into pornography. Do you ever feel that way? How can I help you with that?
- » In what ways am I defensive about my pornography use?
- » Some spouses notice a change in their partners' behavior when they are struggling with pornography. What do you notice in me?

- » Some spouses feel like their partners' pornography use is their fault. Do you ever feel that way? Can you please tell me about those feelings?
- » Would it help you if I sought assistance for my struggles? What would you like me to do? Would it help if you accompanied me or also sought help?
- » Some spouses feel like pornography is the same as or even worse than infidelity. What are your feelings about this?
- » Some spouses struggle with not being included in their partners' private meetings with their bishops. How do you feel about my meetings with the bishop? Would you like to meet with me and the bishop?
- » What devices or sources are the most tempting to you and why?
- » What is it like for you when you feel out of control of your sexual behavior?
- » When have you engaged in masturbation or stimulating yourself sexually?
- » What were your family's views and teachings about masturbation? How did that affect you?
- » Have you ever felt out of control of yourself with masturbation?
- » How are masturbation and pornography use connected for you?
- » Please tell me, without details, about your previous sexual relationships and how they have impacted your thoughts, feelings, and experiences with sex.
- » How do you believe your past sexual relationships will (or do) affect our relationship?
- » Have you ever had a sexually transmitted disease? Please tell me about that.
- » Do you feel you have any fetishes or odd sexual feelings or urges? Please tell me about those.
- » Have you ever paid for sexual contact online or in person? Please tell me about this.

- » Do you believe I am making excuses or rationalizing my addiction to pornography or other behaviors? In what ways?
- » What behaviors would you like me to change to better help you know that I am working to overcome my addiction?
- » What can I do to earn back your trust after I have betrayed you by my pornography or masturbation habits?
- » What are your thoughts and feelings about participating in the addiction recovery program? Professional counseling?
- » Please tell me about any times or situations where you have been unfaithful to me in thought, word, or action.
- » How do you protect yourself and manage temptation when you are away from home or away from me?

Let's Talk (for parents)
- » Please tell me what you believe pornography is.
- » Please tell me what you believe masturbation is.
- » Have you ever accidentally found pictures or videos of people who were naked or doing other things? Please tell me about those experiences.
- » Have you ever touched or rubbed your body in any way that felt good to you? What do you know and understand about those feelings?
- » What questions do you have about things you have seen or heard online, on your phone, on TV, or at school?
- » I recently found things on the computer or on your phone that are concerning to me. Please tell me about those things you were looking at.
- » Do you ever feel like I do not understand what you face in terms of temptations and the law of chastity? How can I be more supportive and understanding?
- » Some kids hear words or phrases at school, from friends, and even at church that are confusing to them. Some of those words are *masturbation, pornography, chastity, fornication,* and so on. What words have you heard? What questions do you have about anything you have heard or seen?

- » Some kids are afraid to talk to their parents about things they see or hear online, on their phones, or at school. How can I help make it safer and less scary for you to talk to me?
- » Some kids are afraid to ask their parents for help if they are struggling with pornography or other things they see online or on their phones. How do you feel about what you see? How can we better support you?
- » Have you ever been asked to send pictures or videos of yourself to others? How do you feel about that? Have you ever been asked to send pictures or videos of yourself naked or in your underwear? Please tell me about that.
- » Some kids really want their parents to help them with struggles with things online or on their phones. How would you like me to best support you?
- » Some kids feel better after they talk to their bishops about struggles with masturbation or pornography. How do you feel about that? What can we do to make that easier or better for you? How would you feel if I went with you to talk to the bishop?
- » Is there anything about being online or on your phone that causes you to feel out of control, guilty, or bad about yourself? Would you please tell me about those experiences? How can I best support you when this happens?
- » How do you feel about us checking your online activity or your phone?
- » Have you ever hidden your online searches or phone activity from me? What do you feel like you need to hide from me? How can we make this better for you?
- » Some kids find talking or chatting with people online who they do not know exciting. What experiences have you had with this?

Chapter 14
Conversations about Gender and Sexual Identity

LIKE IN PREVIOUS CHAPTERS, THE BEST WAY TO HAVE CONVERSATIONS about gender and identity is to start early and have them consistently. Parents should discuss identity from birth onward. Parents who create loving connections and positively discuss gender and identity help their children have confidence in themselves and their later choices. Even more, parents would do best to focus first on eternal identity and purpose and teach this positively. It is wonderful when individuals can say they have always known they are children of God.

When discussing identity, it is important to not oversimplify or be too narrow in our discussions. One's identity is first a child of God. Then, for this mortal life, the road to discovering who we are is often made up of many complex and interrelated parts of our personality, temperament, experiences, and interests. Identity discussions should first center on our divine identity. Then we discuss other specific characteristics and traits branching out from divine identity.

Attraction is almost always connected to our life experiences. Contrary to the way the world teaches it, attraction is more malleable and changeable than we think. Parents may have experienced something similar to this when they see their child interested in dinosaurs or some other toy; then they notice their child has developed an infatuation with the toy. So parents purchase dinosaur books, toys, and movies, and the child's attraction or interest grows. In some kids, it can become almost obsessive. In other kids, the interest or attraction wears off. This is true for youth and adults as well. What we expose ourselves to influences our attraction. Who has thought someone was attractive but then was repulsed when they later got to know the person? This has surely happened for many of us in reverse as well. Many reminisce of not liking someone at first, even despising them, but then circumstance, experience, or exposure changed those feelings and previously disliked individuals became very attractive. What we find attractive about people changes over a lifetime as well. It is normal to move from outward and physical features to appreciating personalities, kindness, and intelligence.

These ongoing identity conversations should be sensitive and involve more listening than talking. Curiosity about gender, identity, feelings, and attractions needs to be discussed in a safe and nonpunitive environment. Parents should be cautious about their personal reactions and do all they need to do to combat personal prejudices and feelings of discrimination. It is normal for children and youth (and even adults) to be curious, explore, have questions, and want to discuss them with someone. Please do everything you can to create ongoing, safe, and kind conversations. Often a loving parent can help guide a child more by listening and understanding than by preaching or testifying. There is a place for teaching, but that is always best after learning and understanding.

It is often helpful, when discussing identity, to help individuals separate fixed or constant things from changing things. It can be helpful to separate the "I am" from the "I do." All too often these two categories are mixed up. What we do may feel like who we are, but that is not the case. We may say that we are a dancer, musician, or athlete, but those are things we participate in and enjoy. When we separate "I am" from "I do," we often can find better stability in who we truly are. Many of the things on our "I do" lists will drop off over time. Interests and actions change. While what we do changes, who we truly are never changes. We should be careful not to identify ourselves by something we do.

When it comes to discussing identity, it is also essential to not define ourselves by only one aspect of ourselves or experiences. God made us complex and wonderful and unique. There is no one like you on this earth. You are a wonderful composition of all kinds of remarkable attributes, characteristics, and dispositions. How incredible that God made you just as you are! Resist the temptation and the pull of the world to put yourself (or others) in a little box. Healthy individuals have a strong sense of and embrace the many facets of eternal identity and purpose.

In any discussion of identity, it is also important to recognize that certain attributes, interests, preferences, temperaments, and dispositions do not necessarily mean anything. There is room for variety in what we prefer, what we pursue, and what we love. There are sensitive and tender men (Jesus Christ surely was one!), and there are tough and serious men. There are sensitive and tender women, and there are tough and serious women. Having certain attributes or dispositions does not mean other things are true as well. We should learn to embrace all the good parts of ourselves and make them part of who we are striving to become.

Finally, discussions of identity and purpose do not require immediate action. The world and others may pressure us to immediately respond to all feelings, inclinations, and tendencies. Parents may feel pressured to take some sort of immediate action. Children and youth may feel pressure to act in a certain way or do something right away because of thoughts or feelings. Youth certainly feel incredible pressure to figure out who they are, how they fit in, and where they belong. There is no need to use haste in handling these feelings and thoughts. Life's most important decisions are best made carefully, after much consideration and prayer, and when we are mature and ready.

Experts on identity often encourage parents to take a be-watchful-and-wait approach. This means careful attention, ongoing conversations, and loving support and connection. Make every effort to have a strong and stable relationship. Research has clearly shown that strong relationships are the best foundations for all of us. That is where we should start. *Being watchful* means being attentive and responsive. It means being available to answer questions, resolve concerns, provide guidance and support. Most children and youth make it successfully through those years of uncertainty, exploration, curiosity, and peer pressure just fine. When parents are loving guides on the side, providing gentle teaching with ongoing conversations, this can be a wonderful time.

Adults should also consider taking a watch-and-wait approach. Again, major life decisions and choices—especially around identity—are best explored with patience and time. As we traverse the varying seasons of life, it is normal to experience questions and struggles about who we are and what our lives mean. When these events come, explore them with wisdom and do not be too quick to make major changes. Even more, we must be extra careful about rewriting the past, looking back, drawing conclusions about prior events, and changing life narratives when facing questions of identity. Stay on the solid foundation of divine identity and work from there. A patriarchal blessing can be an essential guide in these moments to recall who you are and what your eternal identity and purpose is all about.

In all cases, individuals and family members should do everything they can to address other concerns and issues that may be occurring at the time. If there is depression, anxiety, or some other concern, it should be treated by competent professionals. If there are significant struggles with abuse, eating disorders, or other major challenges, these should be addressed early and first. Parents, teachers, and leaders should be sensitive to all signs of bullying or mistreatment and address them immediately. All other concerns and impacts should be addressed before making decisions about identity. Again, important decisions should be made from a place of strength. Individuals should get the help they need with any concerns or struggles before making any significant life changes.

Finally, we can all do better at being loving and accepting of everyone. We should do all we can to root out any personal prejudices or hard feelings for anyone. The first and second commandments involve loving God and our neighbor. We all need to make sure love is our first goal. All of us need to know we are loved. We especially need that love when we are struggling with questions of identity and purpose. We need that love when the world is shouting many different and confusing messages. We need to know we are children of heavenly parents who love us. We need to know we are loved here on earth. We can all get better and be better at loving others. This is always the first, middle, and last thing we should do.

Let's Talk
- » How do you feel about being first a child of God? How does that impact every other part of you?
- » What parts of you and your identity do you believe are fixed and unchanging?
- » What parts of your personality and identity would you like to build on or grow?
- » What parts of who you are do you like?
- » What parts of you do you not like?
- » Do you ever feel like there is a conflict between who you feel you are and what you want?
- » Many feel pressure from others to be certain things or accept certain things about themselves. What pressures have you felt? How can I help you work through those pressures?
- » Where do you think your sexual feelings fit within your personality and identity?
- » What messages have you seen or heard recently that cause you to question your identity or personality?
- » Many people question identity at certain times in their lives. When did that happen to you? What was that like?
- » Many people question their identity in the middle of other emotional, mental health, or social struggles. What things are going on for you that might be contributing to questions about identity?
- » What are your feelings about sexual orientation?
- » How important do you think it is to declare a sexual orientation or make your sexual feelings and orientation known? What factors contribute to how you feel about this?
- » There are many mixed messages about what makes up sexual orientation (such as interests, preferences, temperament, and more). What messages are you hearing, and how do they affect your feelings?

- » It helps some people to view their identity like a pizza with many different slices. Would it help you if we looked at all the different parts of who you are?
- » What experiences have you had with people of different genders? How do those affect you and your feelings and beliefs?
- » What experiences have you had with people of different sexual orientations? How do those affect you and your feelings and beliefs?
- » Have you ever been bullied, discriminated against, or mistreated because of parts of your feelings, preferences, identity, or manner of expressing yourself? How does that affect you now?
- » How do you feel about teachings of the Church that say there are only two genders—male and female?
- » How do you feel about Church teachings that say that sexual expression is only permitted between a woman and man who are married to each other?
- » How do you feel about Church teachings regarding marriage only being permitted between a man and a woman?

Chapter 15
Addressing Children and Youth at Church

TEACHERS IN THE CHURCH OF JESUS CHRIST OF LATTER-DAY SAINTS, especially those who teach children and youth, have a great opportunity to help with conversations about sex. In these callings, we are the best resource available to parents to help them in their responsibility to educate their children on this important topic. We should be careful to never take over the role of parents. However, our assisting role can be very helpful.

We should be familiar with teaching resources already available to us to teach and answer questions about sex and other related topics. As professionals, we get asked all the time, "How come the Church does not have anything on . . . ?" Our most common response is to direct them to ChurchofJesusChrist.org or the Gospel Library app. There are countless resources to help you teach, answer questions, and support families when there are questions related to sexual intimacy. Too many times we look only to professionals and experts to answer questions. However, your personal relationship with children and youth makes you the perfect person to help.

First, lessons and discussions on the law of chastity need to emphasize more than restrictions and limitations. Make every effort to emphasize teaching the doctrines and principles connected to this beautiful law. If you are married, you are in a unique position to bear testimony of the beauty and wonder of a temple marriage and the sacred expressions of intimacy within marriage. Of course, you should not share any details, but you should testify and be an example of how amazing love can be. When you speak of arriving at the temple clean and pure, kneeling across a sacred altar, and experiencing tender expressions of love and connection, you create a picture of what can be for them. We spend too much time talking about what is not okay and too little time talking about what is wonderful! Make sure you create a vision for where they are headed, and this will help them answer the rest of their whys. Frame every question in the context of the doctrine and beauty of eternal marriage and becoming like our heavenly parents. We spend too much time batting around questions of "How come we can't . . .," "Is it okay to . . .," and "What does _____ mean?" We need to spend more time talking about, testifying of, and feeling the sacredness of marital intimacy. If your class is trying to figure out where the line is, you are probably not focused on the right direction. Set their sights on the ultimate goal and the wonder of it. This always helps answer all the other questions. Follow the pattern of teaching correct principles and allowing them to take it from there.

Talk confidently to children and youth of all ages about eternal identity and purpose. Never shy away from talking about the divine roles of men and women, our eternal and shared purposes, and the beauty of it all. Try to always help children and youth connect to their eternal identities, their covenant identities, and their roles as disciples of Jesus Christ. At every possible opportunity, remind them of who they are, why they are here, and that they are special. Help them make connections to covenants and ordinances, and testify of how special it is to be a covenant keeper. If you have made those covenants, testify of how they have impacted your personal identity, confidence, worth, and joy. Help them understand that God has made us all unique and special for the accomplishment of His divine purposes for us and others. Our uniqueness makes us special, and our covenant connection to Him magnifies that in every way. Help each of them embrace the unique parts of who they are, connecting it to their eternal identities and purpose. Never hesitate to bear testimony about the divine role of men and women, families, and sacred covenants. Even the youngest of children can feel the Spirit through your testimony.

Finally, as a teacher and leader of children and youth, you will have many opportunities to influence them for good as you interact with them outside of the classroom. They will look to you as a model and an example. If you look for opportunities and strive to be prepared, you will be able to point out unique strengths and attributes. You will be placed in such a way that you can help them see their talents and connect them to their worth and identities. You will be able to have conversations about things that are meaningful to them and influence them with your simple testimony of the goodness of God, His divine plan for them, and the importance of temple marriage. Seek to be in tune with the Spirit. Remove distractions and find ways to be with those you teach, to talk to them, and to encourage them. Be a good listener, and seek to understand their questions and thoughts. Then share your own relevant experiences.

You can trust that the Lord has called you and will put you in a place where you can help if you listen and look for opportunities. Make sure you are grounded firmly in gospel truths so you can help the children and youth you teach find their own answers. Your guidance and testimony will help them. Be careful about getting into deep discussions, and always follow Church policies about interactions and relationships with youth. Be a model. Be an example. Be a strong advocate for marriage, the wonder of the law of chastity, the divine roles of men and women, and eternal identity and purpose. As you are confident in who you are, who called you, and your divine role and purpose, you will teach them by the way you live, the way you speak, and who you are.

Let's Talk
- » What kinds of messages are you getting about sex, sexual orientation, and chastity at school? On social media? From your friends?
- » How do you feel about the messages you get from these sources?
- » What are some of the confusing messages you are hearing or seeing about sex?

- Many people struggle with people saying the Church is insensitive or unfair to people with different sexual preferences or gender expressions. How do you feel about that?
- What are the biggest pressures you face when it comes to matters of chastity and virtue?
- Sometimes youth feel like parents and Church leaders are vague, confusing, or unclear about matters of sex, gender, and chastity. What are you confused or unsure about?
- What sexual terms or words are you unsure about?
- What parts of the standards for youth are confusing to you or you feel like you do not understand?
- Many young people wonder if it is okay to have friends who are LGBTQ+. Some even feel guilty or like they are doing something wrong. Have you ever felt this way? What was that like for you?
- Teenagers often describe intense sexual feelings. What is that like for you?
- Sometimes sexual feelings can be confusing. How are they confusing for you?
- The world seems to be focused on sex, sexuality, sexual identity, and sexual expression. How have you felt pressure to declare a sexual preference or to take a stand on matters of sexuality?
- Many youth have mixed feelings and confusion about gender, sexual identity, and sexual feelings. When have you felt that way? How did you resolve that?
- Many young people feel like they cannot talk about matters of sex with their parents or leaders. How do you feel about that? What would make that easier for you?
- What do you believe about attraction?
- What do you believe about gender and gender identity?
- What are the greatest pressures you face when it comes to gender and sexuality?
- Sometimes youth are confused about pornography, what it is, and how it makes them feel. What questions do you have about pornography and how it affects you?

- » Some people assert that in matters of sexual preference and identity, we are born that way. How do you feel about that?
- » Where do you turn when you have questions about sex, sexuality, gender, and identity? What has that experience been like for you?
- » What do older people like parents and Church leaders not understand about younger people and the challenges and experiences they are facing when it comes to sex, sexuality, sexual expression, and gender?
- » What are the hardest parts for youth today about living the Lord's law of chastity?

Chapter 16
The Bishop: Leading the Ward in Matters of Sex and Chastity

THANK YOU FOR YOUR FAITHFUL AND DEVOTED SERVICE AS A BISHOP! We are grateful for you and the great work you do for so many! You are in a position of great trust, especially when it comes to handling matters related to sex and the law of chastity. You can do so much good to help people get on the covenant path and stay on it. You are also in the position of helping those who have wandered off the path make their way back. You are called of God.

As the bishop, you can set the tone for the ward by how you teach and testify about things like marriage, the law of chastity, the divine roles of men and women, eternal identity and purpose, and living covenant lives as disciples of Jesus Christ. You are the one who oversees and plans the teaching of doctrine, correct principles, and the pure truths of the gospel of Jesus Christ. As you fulfill this sacred role, please make sure that sacrament meetings, Sunday lessons, youth and primary activities, and other events (fifth Sunday lessons, firesides, youth councils, etc.) are planned in such a way that helps all connect to their eternal identities and purpose and the power of covenants. Please ensure you and other ward leaders never shy away from teaching the divine roles of men and women. In a world that seeks to blend and erase these roles, where else but at home and church will our people hear these essential messages? When the internet and the world are blasting messages that confuse gender, sexual identity, the purpose of sex, and divine roles, the ward needs you to be fearless in ensuring that correct gospel messages are conveyed. Do all you can to connect members to their divine identity as children of God. Then help them know how to make and keep sacred covenants and become disciples of the Lord Jesus Christ.

When members come to you for questions or confessions, your sensitivity and willingness to listen fully for understanding makes all the difference in the world. Professionals often talk about connection before correction. Please make sure you take adequate time to listen and understand before you begin to correct or make judgments. You need to fully understand. A warm and loving relationship with the bishop can be transformative and healing. When it comes to youth who confess to breaking the law of chastity, please take enough time to fully understand the events and circumstances that happened before, during, and after the confessed event to make sure you are responding in the right way. It is not uncommon for young women (and some young men) to confess to a violation of the law of chastity when the event was clearly sexual assault. You need to be sure the incident was a consensual action. Take the time to really understand the scenario. You do not need all the details, but make sure you inquire enough to be sure of what really happened. Much harm comes to abuse victims when leaders treat what happened as a sin rather than a tragedy because they did not get enough information. We need to know enough to make sure we are providing the right remedy.

When an individual demonstrates the courage to come in for conversations about issues involving gender, sexual identity, and law of chastity, please be extra tender and loving as you listen to their questions and concerns. One of the first things individuals often say after contact with their bishop on these sensitive issues is "I wish he would have told me that the Lord loved me and that he loved me." Even more, they will often say things like, "I wish the bishop had given me a hug." Of course, you need to be sensitive and follow Church policies, but remember that these individuals are being vulnerable. They are showing considerable trust in you and the Lord by meeting with you. It takes great faith and courage to be willing to meet with your bishop on such personal matters. Please be extra sensitive when anyone comes to meet with you, especially if it involves matters related to sex and sexuality. These are critical moments in a person's walk along the covenant path. What happens here can shape much of what happens next for them.

As you listen to individuals, please be careful about providing answers for them. It would be better to turn them to the scriptures, the teachings of living prophets, and the gift of the Holy Ghost. You do not need to be the source of all knowledge and have all the answers. In cases of questions and confessions, one of your main duties is to turn them to the Savior. Please remember this. Do all you can to turn them to Him. Help them create action steps to better understand the Lord Jesus Christ and His perfect doctrines. Teach those doctrines boldly and with confidence. Please assure them that all the answers needed are found in His doctrine. Turn them to correct sources, and explore them together. Please use correct and current terms for sexual conduct and misconduct. Please don't confuse people with out-of-date terms like *self-abuse* or *fornication*. Please use current words and terms and be willing to define them for the members with whom you meet (e.g., *masturbation*, *premarital sex*, etc.). For matters of gender, sexual identity, and the law of chastity, please follow the handbook exactly. Don't assume you know. Review the handbook often, counseling with the stake president, and seek direction as needed. If you have a Family Services office in your area, a consultation with a specialist there may be helpful.

When individuals come to you with compulsive sexual struggles, please remember that being harsh, punitive, or abrasive is never helpful. In fact, punishment rarely helps. You may need to consider and implement restrictions, but in all cases remember the goal is to assist the individuals to fully repent and set aside these behaviors. Help them look to the Lord, scriptures, latter-day prophets, and family for answers. Be positive and help them brainstorm ways they can change life patterns and become better. Help them learn from setbacks and relapses and create proactive habits and plans for future temptations. Be an encourager and a coach. Help them implement what they already know, teach them additional truths, and encourage them to act in all diligence. Your effort to coach them to their own answers and cheer them on builds confidence.

Help them look for ways to apply actions such as fasting, prayer, sacrifice, service, and temple and family history work to their efforts. Help them replace the bad habits and patterns with righteous habits and patterns. If they do not appear to be making progress, help them enlist the help of others. This could include family members, elders quorum or Relief Society presidents, ministering companionships, and other trusted friends and associates. Your prayerful assistance in enlisting these individuals is monumental in its effects and follows the Lord's divine pattern for helping each other in higher and holier ways. You should follow this pattern as quickly as possible. You may also want to refer individuals to addiction recovery groups and resources, Family Services, or other trusted professionals in your area. Please engage others' help sooner than later, especially if someone seems stuck or is not making progress. Please never forget to involve parents and spouses. Make sure you spend time with and reach out to them. Be careful to never make spouses or family members feel responsible for their loved ones' struggles. Suggesting that spouses or parents are responsible is hurtful and damaging to individuals, marriages, and families. Offer them support, compassion, and encouragement to care for themselves and their families, and find ways to support the struggler in healthy ways.

When you are helping people navigate the path of repentance, please be optimistic in how you present solutions. As you request action from them, remember to ask for positive actions instead of asking them to stop negative actions. Help them see that engaging in positive habits and patterns is more helpful than simply trying to stop the bad. Help them create plans to act and then follow up with them regularly with encouragement and optimism. Your loving support (as well as the support of those you delegate to) can go a long way in helping them move forward.

Please consider carefully how you conduct interviews. It is appropriate to ask individuals if they prefer to have another trusted person in the room. Please be sensitive in these cases. In other cases, it may be appropriate to ask another trusted leader to join you for the interview. Bishops can delegate more to elders quorum and Relief Society presidents by having them present for important interviews. These leaders can be on hand and invited into the room when appropriate to assist with follow-up and ongoing support. They are your best tools for enlisting the full resources of the ward. Be courageous in asking for permission to involve these leaders. Help people understand that this is the Lord's way of helping His children. You may also want to consider asking individuals coming for interviews to take out their phones and turn them off. You may ask them not to record or share the details of these interviews with others. Remind them of the sacredness of these meetings and how important it is that we feel the Spirit and follow Him. Removing all distractions and interruptions is essential.

In all cases, please remember you are not on this mission alone. Please involve family members, your elders quorum and Relief Society presidents, ministering brothers and sisters, your counselors, the stake president, and others. You will serve others better as you prayerfully seek ways to invite others to serve and help. As you lovingly find ways to surround members of your ward with care and fellowship, you will witness miracles in the lives of many. It is not wise to go it alone. There are certain areas for which you are to be the judge and the witness, but there are many more ways to offer support outside of those things. Please be wise in enlisting all the help you can.

Please remember that all issues that involve abuse should be handled according to the directions in the Church's handbook. Enlist the help of the professionals on the twenty-four-hour abuse help line in every case of reported or suspected abuse. Follow their instructions on reporting. Ensure that all called teachers and leaders of children and youth complete the abuse training *before* they are permitted to serve in their callings. Consider asking a counselor or another called individual to ensure that all those who have contact with children and youth are trained. It is critical that you take the lead in protecting children and youth. Do not permit exceptions in any way to policies and directions regarding the protection of children and youth.

Finally, a consistent theme throughout this book has been ongoing conversations. You can do much good as a leader as you facilitate and create opportunities for ongoing discussions about the law of chastity and all these related matters. While a youth standards night can be a wonderful evening, it would be better if such nights were followed by ongoing, positive conversations about these things. A fifth Sunday presentation on pornography may provide some good information, but if you really want to help your ward members, please consider ways to have ongoing conversations about the topic. As you work with your ward council and other wonderful members of your ward, you can create plans to follow through with real help. Rarely does a one-time meeting on these topics make much of an impact. Continuing conversations and openness to discussing these topics is key. If you want to make lasting change, start looking for ways to have ongoing dialogue today.

Let's Talk (for bishops)
- » Review all handbook sections carefully for policies and directions in matters of chastity, sexual expression, sexual identity, and gender. Please encourage members to study those sections alone, with you, and with others.
- » Counsel together with the stake president on all matters and questions you have about how you should respond and are responding to sexual and gender issues.
- » Use resources available to you on the Church website and in the Gospel Library app. Become familiar with "Counseling Resources" for suggestions on specific questions you can ask in interviews with members. Also become familiar with sections of "Life Help" for additional information and supportive questions you may ask.
- » Consult with your local Family Services office (if applicable) or your Area Presidency office with questions you may have or how to best structure interviews and visits when issues of chastity are present.
- » Consult with the Church's twenty-four-hour abuse help line to discuss any issues of sexual abuse and how to respond to matters of sexual identity, orientation, or gender. If you are outside of the United States, please consult with your local abuse help line or the area office.

Chapter 17
Establishing Ongoing Conversations with Children about Sexual Intimacy

Surely, at this point, you have captured the importance of having ongoing conversations about sex, sexual intimacy, and all other related topics. While it is important in every other setting, it is crucial in the home. Children's very first lessons on gender, sexual identity, and sexual expression happen in the home. In fact, these lessons begin almost as soon as they are born. Much of what you do and say as individuals and as a couple will teach lessons on these topics. It is important that you start early, be consistent, and create many opportunities throughout your children's lifetimes to talk about the wonderful blessings and joys of the law of chastity.

As you commence this journey, you must understand the law of chastity yourself. Please carefully study the law of chastity individually and together. If you have not yet discovered the beauty, power, and wonder of this beautiful doctrine, then please search for that together. Most of us were not taught this, so we must seek it out ourselves. If you are struggling with issues of chastity and virtue and cannot see the amazing aspects of this doctrine, then please do the personal work to change that view. Talk to each other about it. Pray about it. Search the scriptures. Study "The Family: A Proclamation to the World." Attend the temple, and prayerfully reflect on this sacred covenant and its meaning. Talk to Church leaders or trusted professionals about any concerns or roadblocks you are facing. Repent if needed. Do all you can to make sure you have a powerful testimony of the sacred truths of the law of chastity. It will make all the difference as you help your child navigate this world.

The human body is amazing and wonderful! God truly created something of wonder when He created us. Our bodies can do remarkable things. This is especially true when it comes to our sexual and procreative powers. When it comes to speaking about the body, it is critical that you use correct terms for anatomy including (and especially) the private parts of our bodies. Most of us were not raised using these terms directly. Some of us had parents who gave nicknames to private parts. It is essential that you become comfortable with and use the proper terms to refer to your body and your child's body.

Using the correct terms for our bodies helps children and youth fully understand the function of the various parts of their bodies. Even more, when we teach and use correct terminology, we eliminate any kind of shame about who we are and the wonderful bodies we inhabit. Let us do more to celebrate the amazing aspects of our bodies without creating feelings of embarrassment, humiliation, or shame. Children should never be shamed for being curious about their bodies and all their parts and functions. Make sure you are using proper and current terminology, and be willing to define or explain any terms your child does not understand. Children who feel safe exploring their body are more likely to be open to you when they have questions, concerns, or new experiences. We want to build openness and comfort from the beginning.

Children need help to explore how their bodies work, and parents are the primary source of information (or at least we should be!). If you are married, it is important that both of you be involved in these ongoing conversations and discussions. When children learn from both their mothers and fathers about the specialness of their bodies, they build a solid foundation for their entire life. Please consider again getting your own appropriate sex education. It can be helpful to understand the phases of physical and sexual development. When you pair that knowledge with greater understanding of intellectual and emotional development, you have power. For example, when you have a firm understanding of normal development, you would know a young child exploring the private parts of the body is just being curious. You would never label that as a sin and punish or shame them. A firm testimony of the law of chastity combined with adequate knowledge enables us to better handle the normal parts of curiosity and growth. All too often children and youth are shamed for being normal and curious. We need to be educated from the best resources on what is normal so we can help our children navigate in healthy ways. The more open, calm, and prepared we are, the better we will handle the questions and challenges that may come.

We need to have conversations early on and consistently about the different phases and stages of physical and sexual development. Both mothers and fathers need to understand normal development for both sons and daughters. Both parents need to be prepared to talk calmly and with understanding about the changes that come. We need all hands on deck to handle these changes with love and proper teaching. A parent who will not talk about these things and sends the child to the other parent is not only missing a special opportunity, but also might be sending hurtful messages about gender, sexuality, and normal development. These conversations are ones to be sought after, prepared for, and excited about. Strive to be ready to celebrate the wonderful changes that will come for your child. A father who honors and celebrates his daughter's first period can do much to help her accept and love herself. A mother who responds similarly to her son's development can make a huge impact. Work together to be excited about what is happening.

Do all you can to never shame children for being curious (at any stage) and wanting to know more. When they know either one or both of you are receptive to conversations about bodies, their functions, odd things that happen, and rapid changes, they will be more willing to talk to you and seek your advice. Children are blessed when, in an ideal home, both mothers and fathers lovingly talk about and model respect and appreciation for their bodies and the sacred law of chastity. We can do much good when we embrace the wonder of our bodies and the powers and blessings God has bestowed and pass that on to our children. Single parents should be creative in enlisting the help of grandparents, ministering brothers and sisters, and others to help teach all aspects of gender, sexuality, and the law of chastity.

Parents need to understand that over the course of our lifetimes, we all have important same and opposite sex needs. Again, in an ideal home, a child is exposed to gender and differences related to gender. This helps teach a child about the many aspects and wonders of gender and identity. Over their lifetimes, children will explore different aspects of their personalities, interests, and temperaments. It is not unusual or of concern when a child favors one gender over the other. It is not uncommon for children to surround themselves with same-sex peers for a time and then become interested in opposite-sex peers at another time. Even more, parents often enjoy the sweet moments when a daughter adores her dad or a son adores his mom. Then we feel sad when that special closeness changes and transfers to the other parent. When children go through normal phases of liking and disliking people of different genders, parents should expect and embrace it. We can do much to encourage our children to associate with others and learn from them. We should not punish them or restrict them but see this as a healthy part of growth and development. We should also do all we can to help them not develop prejudices, discriminate against, or be hurtful in any way to anyone or any group because of gender, sexual orientation, and so forth.

Additionally, it would be wise to actively challenge outdated and inappropriate attachments of certain activities, temperaments, preferences, or interests to a specific gender or ideal. Candidly speaking, these stereotypes and notions that only one gender owns certain attributes, characteristics, temperaments, and so forth are destructive to children and youth. There is room for all of us to explore the things we are interested in and want to pursue. We should not exclude our children from participating in things because we hold an outdated belief that they should not be doing that activity or have those interests or sensitivities. We should check our own wishes and preferences for our children and their interests and activities at the door and help them fully explore what they find interesting and exciting. For instance, if our young toddler boy wants to play with dolls or our teenage daughter wants to join the football team, we can be excited they found something they enjoy. We can celebrate what this shows us about them and who they are becoming. Even more, we should never shame, punish, or degrade children for their temperaments, sensitivities, emotional makeups, or anything else about their personalities. To be hurtful to children because they have different personalities, temperaments, or interests than what you hoped for, expected, or wanted is unacceptable. It denies the unique nature that each of us brings into the world by virtue of our premortal lives, our eternal identity and purpose, and who we are destined to become. It is abusive and should not be tolerated by us, extended family members, or anyone else. Do all you can to protect your children from being shamed for who they uniquely are. Provide them with opportunities to explore who they are, and be curious and encouraging of their choices.

Conversations about body functions, sex, procreation, and so forth should happen early and be ongoing. Consider the age, maturity, and emotional sensitivity of the child when having these discussions. Both parents should be involved in presenting information and answering questions. As you remember that conversations will be ongoing, do not feel you need to cover everything the first time you discuss this. Help your children know that you want to talk to them about their bodies and all their wonders throughout their lives. Some parents choose to be more formal with scheduled family council meetings. Other parents strive to be informal and seize moments as they come. It is best to consider a combination of both approaches. When parents can create planned moments to educate, instruct, and help, then utilize those spontaneous moments, they provide a culture of safety and openness to questions about sex. As stated earlier, pornography, masturbation, and so forth should be addressed early and regularly. Frankly, conversations about bodies, sex, sexual intimacy, and media portrayals need to be a part of a steady diet of the things we discuss in our homes. In today's world, there is much to talk about. Create a culture where family members can discuss all matters related to chastity and virtue.

When it comes to media, parents should be alert, informed, and careful about the media they allow children to access. Most experts on the topic suggest that young children should not have unsupervised access to electronic devices and computers until they are eight years old or older. Young children do not have the maturity to handle the unlimited content and access phones, computers, tablets, and more provide. They are also not mature enough to understand what they are viewing, and unsupervised childhood curiosity can result in serious problems. Even more, children and youth should not be given electronic devices to manage mood or emotions. When children and youth learn to turn to electronic devices when in negative moods, they never learn to manage their own emotions. We should be wise and careful about when and how we allow children to use electronics and media.

The best approach is a gradual introduction to electronic devices and media. At the start, children should get little access with high parental support and engagement. As they demonstrate maturity and trust, children can be given more access with decreasing parental involvement. Young children (and many youth) do not have the ability to regulate themselves, so we must do that for them. As their ability to handle themselves matures, we can increase things like time and access for them. If there are concerns, we can cut back. An ongoing pattern of increasing (or decreasing) access connected to decreasing (or increasing) parent involvement is the wisest approach. We adapt to the growing abilities and maturity of our children, always there to guide them along the way. Do this with positive support, addressing questions and concerns openly, and with the explicit goal of allowing them trusted access.

Just as a child would never be trusted to take the family car out on his or her own without training, supervision, maturity, and demonstrated trust, we should be careful guides to our children when we grant them access to electronic devices and media of all types. Each child possesses different levels of maturity, interest, and ability to self-regulate, so parents need to be prepared with a family plan that can be adapted to each child. Work together and create openness about discussing anything a child is seeing, feeling, or experiencing. Conversations about how we feel when we see, access, and participate in various forms of media can help children understand themselves and learn self-control. It is better to help children explore their feelings about what they saw, identify those feelings, and express them than to punish them for seeing or accessing something they should not have. Help them learn to listen to their feelings when they use devices and media so they can learn to make better choices.

Children will not learn how to use social media appropriately without proper teaching, loving guidance, and help to get up when they fall. Be a guide on the side, and help them choose wisely how to use their devices and media. If you are among the many adults who are also struggling with access to media and devices and not managing yourself and your emotions, you would benefit from working on this yourself. Parents who model responsible media and technology use and are actively working on it can be an incredible blessing to their children. Make sure you are in control and not accessing your device and media excessively or inappropriately or to regulate your moods. You cannot help the special children entrusted to you if you are stuck on a video game, social media site, or other diversion. Families should create device and media plans and work together in positive ways to make good media and device choices.

Engaged parents have much power to influence their children for good when it comes to virtue and chastity. The best teaching happens in a safe, positive, and nonpunitive environment. When parents welcome questions, keep conversations open and ongoing, and provide proper teaching with love, children and youth become powerful and confident. We can help our children understand, love, and embrace the law of chastity and all the beauty it holds for them. When they can envision making sacred covenants of chastity and virtue in the house of the Lord, we have prepared them for the most amazing experiences and blessings in time and eternity.

Let's Talk
- » How do you feel about your body?
- » What do you like about your body?
- » What parts (if any) of your body do you not like or struggle with?
- » What have you noticed about your body recently?
- » What changes have you noticed in your body?

» Parts of our body can feel good when rubbed against something or touched. Have you noticed this? What was that like for you?
» Sometimes people feel bad or guilty when it feels good to touch parts of their body. Has this ever happened to you? What was that like?
» It is common to see things that are confusing online, on phones, from friends, on television, or in movies. Has that ever happened to you? What was that like?
» Some young people are afraid of getting in trouble for seeing things online, having questions about things they see online, or having conversations with others about sexual things. Has that ever happened to you? What would make it less scary for you?
» Sometimes there are many vague and confusing messages about our bodies, sexual feelings, and sex. What questions do you have? What terms, messages, or feelings have you been confused about?
» Some kids have had experiences with other kids, siblings, family members, adults, teachers, or leaders that were confusing or scary. Has that ever happened to you? What was that like for you?
» Some families like having a family safety plan or communication plan for handling media, technology, and other questions together. How would you feel if our family had a plan? What would you like to be included in that plan?
» What does the word *puberty* mean to you?
» Many people are worried about the changes that normally happen in our bodies as we get older. What do you worry about?
» Many people learn some things about sex at school, from friends, or online. What are you learning or hearing? What questions do you have?

- » Sometimes our friends and others pressure us to share things about our bodies and experiences, and they may even ask for pictures. Has that ever happened to you? How did you handle that?
- » What kind of questions do you have about your body right now? What changes have happened that make you wonder, worry, or nervous? What is confusing about what is happening in your body right now?
- » What are your biggest worries and fears about dating?
- » What questions do you have about handling dating and any pressures to be physical on your date (e.g., holding hands, kissing, etc.)?
- » Some youth feel a lot of pressure to do more physically than they want to when dating or being alone with someone. Has that ever happened to you? What was that like for you?
- » How can we make it safe for you to come to us with questions about sex, your body, and your feelings?
- » What have you learned about the changes that happen for a young woman when she hits puberty or becomes a woman? What questions do you have? Would you like to learn more?
- » What have you learned about the changes that happen for a young man when he hits puberty or becomes a man? What questions do you have? Would you like to learn more?
- » Youth can sometimes bully or tease when it comes to puberty and our bodies. What has it been like with your peers at school and in other places?
- » Many young people think about sexual things and feelings a lot. What is that like for you?
- » Many young people feel extreme shame or guilt for having sexual thoughts or feelings. What has that been like for you?
- » Many young people don't want to date and do not have strong sexual urges, thoughts, or impulses. What has this been like for you?
- » Sometimes sexual urges, appetites, feelings, and impulses can feel overpowering or overwhelming. What has this been like for you?

- » Many young people feel like there is no one to talk to about their sexual feelings and what is okay and is not okay. What can we do to make that safer and easier for you?
- » Many young people wonder if they have done something that means they need to talk to the bishop. Has that ever happened to you? How do you think you could know if you need to talk to the bishop about something?
- » Many youth experience intense pressure from their boyfriends, girlfriends, and others to do things sexually. Sometimes people have even felt forced to do something with someone else. Has that ever happened to you? What was that like?
- » Have you ever wondered if you were sexually abused or assaulted? What happened that made you wonder or worry about that?
- » It is normal to feel weird and awkward talking to your parents about things like sex. How can we make that easier for you?
- » We want to talk to you about any and all questions you may have about your body, your feelings, your attractions, and all other things related to sex and chastity. How can we make sure that happens and that it is comfortable for all of us?

Let's Talk Resources for Parents
- » *https://acpeds.org/position-statements/media-use-and-screen-time-its-impact-on-children-adolescents-and-families* This website reported that teens ranked the internet as #2 source of information about sex with the #1 source being school.
- » *https://www.commonsensemedia.org/sites/default/files/research/report/2023-cs-smartphone-research-report_final-for-web.pdf* This website is fascinating. Not so much about sex but intriguing study about phone use with kids. Since the internet is the second most common resource for kids to learn about sex, it is important that parents understand how their children are utilizing technology.

About the Authors

AMY C. JACOBS, OTD, OTR/L, ENJOYED HER FIRST CAREER AS a full-time mother. Her greatest blessing came from raising her children and being with them to experience all their firsts. She has a bachelor's degree in English from Brigham Young University and a doctorate in occupational therapy from Creighton University. She received specialized training at the Mayo Clinic to work in geriatrics. She loves to help individuals realize greater independence, discover optimal functioning, and get the most out of life. Amy enjoys traveling, eating tacos, and studying beautiful places throughout the world.

JIM R. JACOBS, LCSW, CDWF, LOVES BEING A FATHER MORE than any other role or opportunity. Coming home to family is his greatest joy. Jim has a bachelor's degree in psychology from the University of Northern Colorado and a master's degree in social work from Brigham Young University. Jim has worked in various roles for Family Services for over twenty years. He is the author of two books, *Driving Lessons for Life: Thoughts on Navigating Your Road to Personal Growth* and *Driving Lessons for Life 2: On the Road Again to Better Living, Loving, and Leading.* He is a featured contributor for BizCatalyst 360° where he provides Driving Lessons for Life and other helpful content. He is a Certified Daring Way Facilitator in the work of Dr. Brené Brown. Jim enjoys writing, eating tacos with Amy, and going anywhere she wants to travel.

Appendix A
Speaker-Listener Technique

THE SPEAKER-LISTENER TECHNIQUE IS TAUGHT BY MARRIAGE EDUCATORS and marriage counselors throughout the world to help couples have important conversations in a better way. While there are variations of the technique, the general pattern is described below.

The couple chooses a time and location for the conversation. Some couples also choose a time limit for the conversation, since the goal is to have ongoing conversations throughout the relationship. Some couples choose to have notepads available to record messages they heard and to help them stay focused.

The couple should designate which partner will speak first. This is the speaker. The other partner becomes the listener. Each has important roles to fill. Later, you will switch. The goal is for each to be heard. Couples who practice patience, charity, and love often enjoy this turn-taking approach because it ensures both get the chance to speak and both feel heard and understood.

The speaker's job is to share thoughts, feelings, ideas, perspectives, and preferences in a nonthreatening way without "you" statements or blame. Messages should begin with an "I" statement that communicates your experience. The speaker should be positive and express any feelings, concerns, or needs. The speaker should strive to be kind and gentle and explain only his or her point of view. He or she should make every effort to request positive actions in a kind way. Charity and love guide the conversation as the couple counsels together in loving unity.

The listener's job is to learn and understand. The listener might try to think like a journalist with the goal of getting the story. In all important communication, understanding precedes any generation of solutions, compromises, or changes. A good listener may take notes of key things said to stay focused and not get distracted by any internal dialogue or defensiveness. The listener should take moments to paraphrase, restate, or ask respectful questions about what the speaker has said. Statements like "What I heard you say is . . ." can be helpful. A genuine interest in your partner's point of view is essential. Strive to be charitable and understand the speaker's point of view. Once the listener can restate what he or she has heard to the satisfaction of the speaker, the couple may switch roles. They repeat the above instructions until both feel heard and understood.

This strategy feels a bit awkward at first, but most couples who learn and practice the speaker-listener technique for important conversations report that it provides safety and structure to loving conversations and helps them achieve better understanding. That shared understanding then helps them create loving solutions and make progress together.

Appendix B
Suggested Works of Dr. Brené Brown

WE HIGHLY RECOMMEND THE FOLLOWING BOOKS BY DR. BRENÉ Brown. Many enjoy reading them in this order:
- *The Gifts of Imperfection*
- *Daring Greatly*
- *Rising Strong*
- *Braving the Wilderness*
- *Dare to Lead*

Dr. Brown has also been featured on various media. There are too many to name, but you may wish to look for her in the following places:
- TED Talk: "The Power of Vulnerability"
- TED Talk: "Listening to Shame"
- Netflix: *The Call to Courage*
- Max: *Atlas of the Heart*

An internet search of Dr. Brené Brown will also help you locate forums and interviews with Oprah and other celebrities.

Appendix C
Helpful Resources

HERE IS A LIST OF HELPFUL RESOURCES. PLEASE CREATE YOUR OWN list and be active in seeking out the best books, apps, and websites.

Books

- *And They Were Not Ashamed* by Laura M. Brotherson
- *Knowing Her Intimately* by Laura M. Brotherson
- *From Honeymoon to Happily Ever After* by Laura M. Brotherson
- *The Man's Guide to Women* by John and Julie Gottman
- *She Comes First* by Ian Kerner
- *Come as You Are* by Emily Nagoski
- *The Five Love Languages* by Gary Chapman
- *The Seven Principles for Making Marriage Work* by John Gottman
- *Getting the Love You Want* by Harville Hendrix
- *Hold Me Tight* by Sue Johnson
- *Saving Your Second Marriage before It Starts* by Les and Leslie Parrott
- *How to Talk to Your Child about Sex* by Linda and Richard Eyre
- *A Better Way to Teach Kids about Sex* by Laura M. Padilla-Walker, Dean M. Busby, Chelom E. Leavitt, and Jason S. Carroll
- *Teaching Your Children about Sex* by Cherri Brooks

Apps

- Gottman Card Decks
- Ultimate Intimacy
- Love Nudge
- Intimately Us for Couples
- Focus on the Family

Websites

- GottmanConnect.com (Gottman Relationship Advisor)
- MaritalIntimacyInst.com (specifically this resource: maritalintimacyinst.com/wp-content/uploads/Characteristics-of-Healthy-and-Unhealthy-Sexuality-Raising-the-Bar.pdf)
- Marriage365.com
- FocusontheFamily.com
- TheDatingDivas.com

Appendix D
Choosing a Helping Professional

CHOOSING A PROVIDER CAN SOMETIMES BE SCARY FOR MEMBERS OF The Church of Jesus Christ of Latter-day Saints. This is especially true when we are searching for professionals to assist us with our relationships and vulnerable topics like sex. We all know much of the world does not follow or even respect our values and how we view relationships. We should be careful and discriminating when choosing counselors, occupational therapists, and other providers to assist with issues and questions around sex and sexual intimacy. We should also be strong and courageous advocates for our beliefs, values, and wishes. A provider should never be permitted to impose his or her values, opinions, or perspectives on us. Any provider who pressures, belittles, or tears down your faith may need to be fired and possibly even reported to their licensing board.

When choosing a provider, many members of The Church of Jesus Christ of Latter-day Saints want to choose someone who is also a member of the restored Church of Jesus Christ. While this can be nice, we must continue to be careful and wise in choosing a provider even when they are members of the Church. It is not wise to simply choose someone because they are a member of the same church. That may be something we desire, but it is essential to look at specialties, certifications, and experience. Just because someone is a member of the same church does not mean he or she has any experience with the challenges you are facing. It is wise to consider much more than Church membership as a factor in selecting a provider. More importantly, there are many wonderful providers who provide great care and are not members of the Church. Be wise and discriminating in selecting and using providers. Always advocate for yourself and your faith after you have chosen a provider.

Here are some questions you may wish to ask potential providers:

- » Please tell me a little bit about your experience and how you approach treating . . .
- » Please give me some examples of how you might handle . . .?
- » Please tell me about your approach in helping with . . .
- » Your online profile says you are a Christian. How do you feel about working with Latter-day Saints? What experiences have you had with The Church of Jesus Christ of Latter-day Saints?
- » What is your approach in addressing issues when there are strong religious beliefs, teachings, and convictions attached to them?
- » How do you handle spiritual matters and convictions in your work?